Praise for
The Minimalist Home

"If you are already tapped into the minimalist movement or want to get more in-depth knowledge and know-how, this is the book for you! Joshua Becker takes you through all the benefits and strategies for creating your minimalist home, and he includes practical step-by-step tactics and checklists to create and maintain your spaces. Most importantly, you will gain a complete understanding of the value that minimalism brings to you and your family."

—ELLEN R. DELAP, certified professional organizer and productivity consultant; president of the National Association of Productivity and Organizing Professionals

"Joshua Becker's idea of minimalism is to create a comfortable, warm, inviting home that reflects what is most important to your family. *The Minimalist Home* is a great guide to help you define your vision and set your goals for how you want to live in your space. Joshua goes further than most authors to address pets, hobby areas, and outdoor spaces around the home. Throughout this book, he provides practical advice on how to keep family members engaged in the minimizing process now and in the future."

—JACKI HOLLYWOOD BROWN, editor of Unclutterer.com

"Joshua Becker is the best coach I know of when it comes to teaching the skill of decluttering. Not only will his calm, clear voice guide you through the challenging task of getting rid of belongings, but he will also make you feel fabulous for doing so. He does not shy away from tough topics such as downsizing homes, renting versus buying, and adjusting one's lifestyle to fit a space. His enthusiasm is addictive; it's impossible to read this book without tackling your own home—and then you won't want to stop, because as your rooms open up, so will your entire world."

—KATHERINE MARTINKO, senior writer and editor of TreeHugger.com

"Joshua provides great tips on decluttering every room and inspires readers to think deeply about what really makes a house a home."

—FRANCINE JAY, author of *The Joy of Less*

"This isn't just a book about decluttering. It's a book about remembering what the purpose of every room is and making your home feel like the most important place on earth. Less clutter, more heart."

—CAIT FLANDERS, author of *The Year of Less*

"With his signature optimistic and encouraging writing style, Joshua provides a valuable, practical road map for those who are hoping to declutter their homes and take control of their lives."

—KATIE WELLS, founder of WellnessMama.com

"The result of reading and implementing *The Minimalist Home* together as a family is a household filled with fewer distractions and better conversations. Having fewer barriers between us, our family is now sharing more stories and laughs. We've learned that we don't need more things from the store; we need more of each other in our lives. And this book is the guide that got us there."

—MARC AND ANGEL CHERNOFF, *New York Times* best-selling
authors of *Getting Back to Happy*

"It's a bit ironic that I'm recommending you acquire one more thing to explore living more fully by owning less: Joshua Becker's book *The Minimalist Home*. But I am. It's exactly what we all need—a slim read that's packed with all-new information, authentic stories, and tried-and-true solutions to life's relentless clutter. Joshua speaks candidly (and personally!) about the challenge of expanding our lives by minimizing our stuff. *The Minimalist Home* earns every inch. Can you say that about everything else in your home?"

—MARY KAY BUYSSE, executive director of National Association
of Senior Move Managers

"Since 2005 I have been following in Brazil the growth of people's interest in trying to live in a simpler, more practical, and more organized manner. Joshua's clear, instructive book innovatively shows how minimalism can transform the way we live in our homes, increasing our quality of life. I recommend it as essential reading for everyone."

—JOSÉ LUIZ CUNHA, entrepreneur; founder of OZ! Organize Your Life; and creator of Personal Organizer Brazil, the largest event in Latin America for professional organizers

"This book breaks down the decluttering process into easy-to-follow steps. An essential read for any aspiring minimalist!"

—EMMA LOEWE, home editor at MindBodyGreen.com

The
Minimalist
Home

A Room-by-Room Guide
to a Decluttered, Refocused Life

The
Minimalist
Home

JOSHUA BECKER
with Eric Stanford

WATERBROOK

THE MINIMALIST HOME

Details in some anecdotes and stories have been changed to protect the identities of the persons involved.

Hardcover ISBN 978-1-60142-799-1
eBook ISBN 978-1-60142-801-1

Published in the United States by WaterBrook, an imprint of the Crown Publishing Group, a division of Penguin Random House LLC, New York.

WATERBROOK® and its deer colophon are registered trademarks of Penguin Random House LLC.

Library of Congress Cataloging-in-Publication Data
Names: Becker, Joshua, author.
Title: The minimalist home : a room-by-room guide to a decluttered, refocused life / Joshua Becker, with Eric Stanford.
Description: First Edition. | Colorado Springs : WaterBrook, 2019. | Includes bibliographical references.
Identifiers: LCCN 2018014041| ISBN 9781601427991 (hardcover) | ISBN 9781601428011 (electronic)
Subjects: LCSH: Simplicity—Religious aspects—Christianity. | Personal belongings. | Orderliness. | House cleaning.
Classification: LCC BV4647.S48 B429 2019 | DDC 241/.68—c23
LC record available at https://lccn.loc.gov/2018014041

Printed in the United States of America
2019

10 9 8 7 6 5 4 3

SPECIAL SALES
Most WaterBrook books are available at special quantity discounts when purchased in bulk by corporations, organizations, and special-interest groups. Custom imprinting or excerpting can also be done to fit special needs. For information, please e-mail specialmarketscms@penguinrandomhouse.com or call 1-800-603-7051.

Dedicated to my family,
who make home my favorite place to be.

Contents

YOU

SPACES

FUTURE

PART 1

YOU

Minimalism Makeover

Make the most of the most important
place on earth—home.

I shake my head at those home makeover shows that are so popular on TV. You know, a couple who are discontented with their home invite a design expert to come in and evaluate the situation. The couple nervously agree to stretch their budget as far as possible to make as much of a change as they can. Then a renovation team takes over, carrying out repairs and upgrades (there's always an obstacle that arises and creates drama), and after that the designer stages the house with new furniture, store-bought decorations, and this year's color scheme. Finally the homeowners come back for the big reveal and get teary-eyed at their house's new look.

I shake my head because, even though their house may look nicer, the homeowners typically wind up with just as much stuff as they had before, maybe even more. That's all stuff that may be getting in the way of how they want to spend their days more than it's contributing to the pursuit of their goals. I wonder, after the initial dopamine zap from the redecoration, are their lives really any different? Is their home more personal and life giving to them now, or is it just more pleasing to the eye? Or worse, will their renovated home require more time and money and energy for upkeep than it did in its previous form?

Very few of us get picked to be on TV's home makeover shows, yet most of us who have a house or apartment go through something similar with our own homes. We're disappointed in our living space. We've spent a lot of money buying stuff for our home—and a lot of time organizing, cleaning, and maintaining that stuff. And nevertheless, in the rare times we have left to simply enjoy the home, it doesn't feel like the place we really want to live in. What do we do then? If we don't just give up hope, we most likely double down, continuing to look in all the wrong places for help. We pay attention to commercials and visit showrooms and scroll through shopping sites online, and we decide that we need more stuff or better stuff, with a different organizing and decorating plan. And when we take our best shot at making our living space better, it's . . . well, it's somewhat better in some ways, but it still doesn't give fundamental satisfaction or kick off any lasting life change.

What if the problem isn't that we don't own enough stuff or aren't managing our stuff well enough? What if the problem is that we're living in the homes that advertisers and retailers want us to have instead of the homes that deep down we really want and need?

You can help others by sharing *The Minimalist Home* tips on social media by posting or tweeting the tips labeled #minimalisthome you'll find throughout this book.

I'd like to suggest that what the huge majority of people in my own country—the United States—and other countries need if we are going to be content with our homes and start living more fulfilled lives is a minimalist makeover of our homes. Are you willing to come along with me and explore that idea for *your* home—that there is more joy to be found in owning less than we can ever find in accumulating more? I hope you will, because I know from years of experience that by getting rid of the excess stuff in every room, you can transform your home so that you feel not only free from the stress of so much clutter around you but also free to live a life focused on what you want to do with your limited years on this planet.

Consider the benefits of a minimalist makeover of your home:

You don't have to have an interior designer to do this. You don't need a demo-reno team or real estate agent on your side. You don't need a big budget (or any budget, really), and the investment of time you make up front is something you will recoup many times over in years to come.

You just need determination—and some advice to guide you on the way!

Revolution Indoors

Over the first decade of their marriage, Shannan and her husband moved several times. But there was one constant: everywhere they went, they accumulated more and more stuff, and it was never long before a new home began to feel crowded and messy. Shannan didn't like this situation and felt guilty but didn't know what to do about it. She could sense a growing resentment from her husband over the clutter situation too. When company was coming over, she would move things around to give an illusion of neatness, but of course such maneuvers didn't address the root problem that they simply owned too much stuff.

Not much changed until Shannan and her husband went on a trip from their home in the Midwest to Tennessee, where they stayed in a cabin. "With only what we packed for the week, the cabin seemed spacious and comfortable, though it wasn't really that large," she said. "Once we got home from the trip, I wanted that for our home—room to breathe and enjoy ourselves without things in the way."

This was Shannan's *Aha!* moment. Her trigger. Her tipping point.

I have noticed that, for most people, there is one moment when something causes them to undertake a minimalist makeover. I tell in my previous book, *The More of Less,* about my own trigger moment in 2008, when I was frustrated while cleaning out my garage on a Saturday and a neighbor pointed out that I didn't need to own all that stuff.

Have you had your own minimalism *Aha!* moment? Something that has opened your eyes to the clutter issues you face and has pushed you to do something about them? If not, I hope this book will be that friendly shove for you.

SEVEN SURPRISING FACTS THAT REVEAL HOW MUCH WE OWN

1. In the thirty-five richest countries in the world, total material consumption stands at an average of 220.5 pounds per person each day.[1]
2. Americans spend $1.2 trillion annually on nonessential goods.[2]
3. The United States has more than fifty thousand storage facilities—more than the number of Starbucks, McDonald's, and Subway restaurants combined.[3] Currently, there are 7.3 square feet of self-storage space for each person in the nation, so that it is theoretically possible that "every American could stand—all at the same time—under the total canopy of self-storage roofing."[4]
4. Nearly half of American households are spending so much that they don't save any money.[5]
5. Currently, the "12 percent of the world's population that lives in North America and Western Europe accounts for 60 percent of private consumption spending, while the one-third living in South Asia and sub-Saharan Africa accounts for only 3.2 percent."[6]
6. The home organization industry—benefiting from our desperation to try to manage all our stuff—earned retail sales of $16 billion in 2016 and is growing at 4 percent per year.[7]
7. Over the course of an average lifetime, because of all the clutter we live in, we will spend 3,680 hours, or 153 days, searching for misplaced items. Phones, keys, sunglasses, and paperwork top the list.[8]

Shannan's cabin epiphany inspired her to finally take action on what I would call her "stuff problem." As soon as she got home, she signed up for my online course, Uncluttered, and quickly began making progress on her home. She would take out ten or twelve boxes each week. Her husband got in the spirit as well, clearing out machinery and tools from his garage workshop. Their minimalist home makeover was under way.

Eventually the couple got down to some decisions about what to keep and what to toss that were tougher to make. These are the kinds of decisions that cause some people to quit decluttering before they get the full benefit (and they are some of the decisions I'm going to help you make in this book). Their progress slowed for a while, but they kept going and in the end transformed every part of their home through minimizing.

Minimalism isn't about removing things you love. It's about removing the things that distract you from the things you love. #minimalisthome

---

Shannan said, "Our home is now a place where my husband can come home and feel free to pursue his hobbies and for us to be the couple I know we are without fear of resentment or stress from the outside world. A sanctuary of sorts."

But what's remarkable is not just how minimizing has changed how they feel about their house. It's how differently they feel about themselves. (Though I'm really not surprised.)

"To me, it's so not about the stuff anymore," Shannan said. "My husband has changed too. We're bike riding now and spending more time together."

And it goes even deeper than that. "Aside from my relationship with my husband becoming more loving," Shannan added, "I've gone from being a homebody who was afraid of people and what they thought of me to being someone who wants to be a part of things. I'm consciously making efforts to stand among a group of people talking or offering help to a stranger. Looking people in the eyes when I pass them by, connecting. This is really not who I've been my whole life, and I feel more included in life now that I'm letting others in. How can getting rid of stuff do this? It's really amazing."

That's right—how *can* mere minimalism change lives in a fundamental way? It seems like too much to expect. Yet I've seen it happen over and over. Owning less creates an opportunity to live more.

I've been writing my blog (*Becoming Minimalist*), teaching minimalism, and speaking about the joys of owning less with folks at conferences around the world for a decade now. And I've seen repeatedly, more times than I can recall, that there is an almost magical effect when people right-size the quantity of their possessions—in the process, *the people themselves* are changed in positive ways.

So although this book is about doing a minimalist makeover of your home, I'm warning you now that it may also mean making over yourself in a thousand unforeseeable, positive ways.

Means to a Better Life *for All*

I want to mention something before I go any further because, you see, there's something I hate when the term *minimalism* crops up in conversation. What I hate is the misperception that so many people have about minimalism. Many people think of minimalism as a *style* of home, on a par with Colonial homes, Victorian homes, or Southwest adobe homes. A minimalist home, to them, is a boxy white house with almost nothing in it, and if you do happen to find a chair or sofa somewhere, it's going to be really expensive—and good luck feeling comfortable sitting on it! A minimalist home, in this sense, is for people who don't care much about coziness or comfort and definitely don't have kids or pets or hobbies. Such a house might look good in a magazine photo spread, but who wants to live there?

Creating a minimalist home doesn't mean you have to sacrifice your favorite design style—or even your "no-design style" or "frugal living style"—to accomplish it. In my home, for example, we still use my wife's grandparents' old bedroom set. It's anything but modern in design, but it works for us. My wife, Kim, our two kids, and I got rid of a lot of things when we were transforming our home, but we didn't get rid of everything, and we didn't feel every room needed a different look or style than it had before.

What's widely known as minimalism in architecture and interior decoration today is fine as a design style, if you happen to like it, but that's not at all what I'm talking about here. I'm promoting an approach to owning less that you can take regardless of the style of your home. It's not about making an artistic statement or glorifying emptiness. Instead, it's about transforming your home so that you can transform your life.

Minimalism, as I'm referring to it, is not about taking something away from you; it's about giving something to you. My definition of *minimalism* is "the intentional promotion of things we most value and the removal of anything that distracts us from them." As I sometimes like to say, minimizing is actually *optimizing*—reducing the number of your possessions until you get to the best possible level for you and your family. It's individual, freeing, and life promoting. It's a makeover that you can do on your own, in your current house, just by getting rid of stuff.

In battling against misperceptions about minimalism, I sometimes feel like Henry Ford when he was trying to convince the masses that automobiles didn't have to be just for the rich. Except what's available to everybody now—in our affluent age when it is sometimes said we've reached "peak stuff"[9]—is a radical and amazing home makeover courtesy of minimalism. This is an idea whose time has come. Minimalism isn't just for the few who happen to have some spartan quirk in their personalities; it's for everyone. Homes everywhere would benefit from a thoughtful and deliberate reduction of their possessions load.

So that's how I've written *The Minimalist Home*—with everybody in mind.

This book is for you if you're single or married.

It's for you if you are childless, have one or more kids at home, or have an empty nest where your kids and grandkids come back to visit you from time to time.

REDEFINING NORMAL

In 2012, my twelve-year-old son asked me a question that really struck a chord in me. "Why do we have so much stuff?" he said. "We always have so much to clean."

I replied, "It's normal. People just have a lot of stuff."

Days passed. My son was burdened with many chores. My soldier husband was being deployed, so my son also had to help me with his younger sisters.

One day he asked me to come into his bedroom and started showing me pictures of minimalist homes on his computer. He told me that, if he were to have a house when he grows up, it would be minimalist—no clutter and no things on display. Imagine those words coming from a twelve-year-old!

I was intrigued. I did my research and stumbled upon *Becoming Minimalist*, which prompted me to become more aware of the stuff around me. In addition to my twelve-year-old, I had two toddlers at that time and thought it would be nearly impossible for us to live clutter-free. But as I read, I was more and more interested in transforming my mind and my surroundings.

Well, a few years and three military moves later, my life and my home are very different. The home isn't perfect, but we've gotten rid of a *lot* of things—too many to count.

Creating a minimalist home isn't easy, but it's totally worth it. Minimalism isn't just about living with less; it is about living meaningfully. It took me a while to believe that less is definitely more, but I've seen it to be true over and over again in my life.

I'll never forget the day my son asked me his question.

—Michelle, USA

It's for you if you have an apartment, condo, town house, duplex, detached single-family dwelling, cottage, trailer home, cabin, farmhouse, houseboat, or mobile home.

It's for you if you live in the United States, Australia, England, Japan, Canada, South Africa, Brazil, or anyplace else and your home is overcrowded with stuff.

I'm not trying to make you into someone you're not or turn you into some kind of doing-without extremist. You don't have to live in a tiny home or wander the world living out of a backpack. (My family and I don't.) This book is about doing a makeover to *your* home, wherever that home may be and whatever it may be like. Now, after minimizing, you may want to downsize to a smaller place, but you certainly don't have to move in order to enjoy the benefits of home minimalism. You can change your environment and change your life right where you are.

You bought or rented the home you've got for a reason, right? To some extent, you must have liked it, or at least liked what you imagined it would look like after you were done making it your own. Most likely, it's the overaccumulation of goods since then that's keeping it from being what you wanted. So let's address your "stuff problem." And even if you do choose to do some rehabbing or redecorating in addition to uncluttering, that will be easier after you've minimized.

Give yourself the house you've always wished you had. You've already got it! It's hidden underneath all your stuff.

No Place Like It

I grew up in Aberdeen, South Dakota, where author L. Frank Baum lived for a while in his adulthood. Because of living there, I learned from an early age about Baum's most famous work, *The Wizard of Oz*. I'd be surprised if you don't know the story as well. The book was a bestseller from the time its first edition came out at the beginning of the twentieth century. The 1939 film version, starring Judy Garland, is today the third most-viewed movie of all time around the world (behind *Titanic* and *E.T.*).[10] And what's the most famous line from the movie? Click your heels together and say it with me: "There's no place like home."

I know not everyone has positive associations with home. For some, home has been a place where they aren't safe or where they feel cut down instead of being encouraged to grow. Some are ashamed of or hostile toward their home. Sadly, some don't have a home at all.

Despite all this, the concept of home as an ideal of comfort and safety, of acceptance and belonging, is one that resonates with almost everyone. It inspires longing within us, regardless of how closely or distantly our actual homes have aligned with that ideal. We yearn to make our homes better places than they have been before, both for ourselves and for the other members of our household. There really is no place like home. It is the foremost place on earth, our life's HQ.

Of course, the most important part of a home is the people within it, including the interplay of their relationships, how they spend their time in the home, and the dreams they nurture. But it's also true that a house and its contents can affect the family's quality of life either positively or negatively. And so transforming the place can transform the people.

Consider the following benefits of a minimalist home:

- *A minimized home is a better place to come home to.* Without all the clutter, you'll find that your home is more relaxing and less stressful. With fewer things competing for your attention, you'll appreciate more and make better use of what you have. You'll be able to focus more on the people and activities in the home that bring you joy. I know some people fear that minimizing their home will make it feel cold and impersonal, but I assure you, through minimizing, you'll feel more at home than ever. It will be a place you anticipate returning to at the end of every day or relaxing in for a weekend.

- *A minimized home is a better place to go out from.* After you minimize, you'll be buying less stuff and spending less on repairs and maintenance, leaving you with more cash in your bank account— what I call a "minimalism dividend"—that you can use for other purposes. Even more important, because you'll be spending less time and energy cleaning, organizing, and taking care of your possessions, you'll have more time and energy left over for dreaming and planning for the future. With these extra resources, you'll be better prepared to go out into the world, whether it's for a day's work, an evening's entertainment, or a life-changing adventure.

Do you see what a dynamic concept home is? It's all about the flow. For one thing, a home is a safe haven to duck into amid a storm. Yet as John Shedd said, "A ship in harbor is safe, but that is not what ships are built for."[11] So a home is also a port of departure when you're ready to brave the high seas of life again.

Both benefits of home minimalism—the coming home to and the going out from—are important, but it's the second one that gets me more excited. I don't know about you, but I'll take *significance* over *stuff* every time. I want to *contribute* more than to *consume.*

In *The Wizard of Oz,* Dorothy is desperate to get home. This theme has helped the movie stand the test of time. But notice that her time away from home in the Land of Oz is actually more exciting, providing a thrilling experience in which she grows as a person and helps others along the way. (There's a reason why, in the film version, the Oz sequences are in color while the Kansas parts are in black and white.) The lesson in this for us is that life away from home may be scary, but it's full of potential—and a minimized home can prepare us to go out and encounter it more freely and effectively. That's what Shannan and I and so many other everyday minimalists have discovered again and again.

By doing a minimalist makeover of your home, you, too, can set out on a new course toward fulfilling your purpose and potential in life. And for this reason I just *had* to write *The Minimalist Home* for you.

The All-You-Need Book on
How to Minimize at Home

Inevitably, each time I launch my three-times-annually online uncluttering course, someone will post a comment like "Why would anyone need a course on minimalism? It's easy. Just throw out everything you don't need!"

It drives me crazy to see a comment along those lines. True, there *are* some people (a relative few) who need nothing more than the suggestion that they should own less stuff and they can do the rest for themselves. But that's not most of us. Although we have all no doubt tossed out unused stuff from time to time, many of us don't have experience with making a thorough and lasting change in the material circumstances of our home. Even worse, we've been conditioned since birth by the culture we live in to constantly pursue more and more. So a lot of people need or want an easy-to-follow, thoroughly tested how-to guide to carry them through the process of decluttering the home. *This book is that book.* My promise to you is that you'll find it comprehensive, practical, and encouraging.

Here I've brought together all my key teachings on minimalism. Addressing all the usual concerns, I'm also covering the whole home—every space you'll find in a typical home—in methodical fashion. Furthermore, I've loaded it with handy lists, inspiring testimonials, special topics that will help you form your own strategies for minimizing, and other tools to make it valuable for you to turn to again and again.

So if you're going to own only one book on minimalism to make a lasting change in your home and life, this is it! I know I wish that my wife and I had had this book when we were setting out on our own minimalism journey ten years back. It would have made the process so much easier. I'm thrilled to think of what it's going to do for you.

Before I go any further, I want to take a moment and congratulate you for picking up this book and considering the idea of owning less. Minimalism as a movement is taking off worldwide, yet it still remains countercultural, going against the consumerism and materialism that are pervasive all around us. In a society that consistently paints more and more accumulation as the basis for happiness, owning less requires intentionality, courage, and perseverance. You have to overcome your own inertia, make challenging choices, and establish new habits to minimize and stay minimized. It is not easy, but it is one of the best decisions anybody can make. While people who have something to sell to us shout consumption, minimalism softly invites us to reorient our pursuits around the things that matter most.

If you're dissatisfied with your living space, the wonderful news is that you can create the atmosphere you want in the home you already have—and you don't need to get selected for a TV home makeover show to discover it.

I hope you're ready right now to throw out the excess, clean up the mess, say no to stress, and live with less. Because minimizing your home won't be good just for you; it will also be good for your family. And if I may say so, it will be a prophetic sign for the rest of society about looking in a higher place for our values.

Use this book enthusiastically. Share it widely.

I'm honored to be a part of your journey.

Action recommendation: *You'll be learning my method for removing clutter from the home in the next chapter. But if you're so excited that you feel like doing some decluttering right this very moment, go for it! Make a sweep through your home, grabbing easy stuff to get rid of and enjoying a sense of accomplishment immediately.*

2

The Becker Method

Learn how to keep only those things
that have a purpose that aligns with
your life purposes.

A few summers ago, my extended family and I hiked up Harney Peak (recently
renamed Black Elk Peak) in South Dakota—at 7,242 feet of elevation, the tall-
est mountain east of the Rockies. There were fifteen of us, including cousins,
nieces, nephews, and grandparents. We were excited and ready to conquer the
eight-mile trail together.

The kids did fine at the beginning, skipping enthusiastically up the trail.
But soon the hike grew steeper, rockier, and less exciting. The weather, chilly to
start with, eventually became uncomfortably warm. The trail wound back and
forth with not much but pine trees to look at, and all of us began to wonder if
we were getting anywhere.

But every so often, right when the kids were about to give up, the trees
would clear and we'd happen upon a scenic overlook. From each one, we could
see the beautiful granite peak of the mountain—our destination—off in the
distance. We would take pictures, rest briefly, and then, with renewed energy
and resolve, begin again along the trail.

Goals shape us and goals change us. Our goals in life determine the actions we take and how hard we work to reach them. When we know what our

goals in life are, we set our priorities accordingly. And as long as we keep them in sight, we won't be as likely to turn back or lose the trail.

This is why, although the method for minimizing a home that I teach is a very practical one, it is also fundamentally purposeful. It helps us achieve our dreams, goals, and desires. It's not just about freedom from clutter; it's also about freedom for a better life.

A minimized home is a home that is a joy to come home to and an inspiring place to go out from . . . but exactly *how* your home will be so comforting to you and *why* you need it to be a great launching pad back into the wider world is up to you. Whatever your reasons for doing a minimalism home makeover are, it's important for you to be clear on your goals—your "mountaintop." Because there will be times ahead when the path is rocky and steep, and you may feel discouraged and want to quit. In those moments, it will be important to remind yourself of your motivations for owning less.

All fifteen of us made it to the summit of Harney Peak. You, too, can make it all the way to your goals for minimalism. And in fact, from the vantage point on top of that peak, you might be ready to set some even higher goals for yourself.

There are many ways to go about minimizing your home, but if you want a process that is efficient and thorough, produces long-lasting results, and offers benefits that transcend mere tidying up, this is the way to go.

The Becker Method

1. Have goals for your home and your life in mind as you start minimizing.
2. Try to make it a family project, if you live with family members.
3. Be methodical:
   - Start minimizing with easier spaces in the home and then move on to harder ones.
   - Handle each object and ask yourself, *Do I need this?*

- For each object, decide if you're going to relocate it within the home, leave it where it is, or remove it. If you're going to remove it, decide if you're going to sell it, donate it, trash it, or recycle it.
- Finish each space completely before proceeding to the next.
- Don't quit until the whole house is done.

4. As much as you can, have fun with the process. Notice and articulate the benefits that appear along the way. And celebrate your successes.

5. When you're done, revisit and revise your goals, aiming to make the most of your newly minimized home and newly optimized life.

That's the overview—a proven strategy for minimizing a home that anyone can implement and that's wrapped in purpose. Let's look at how to put this method into practice in your home.

Minimal on Purpose

What are your purposes for your home?

What are your purposes for your life after you've minimized your home?

Spend some time thinking about these goals. Discuss them with your spouse or family. You don't have to know definitively what they are right now (in fact, you probably won't), but you can make a start. And if you keep thinking about them, they will become clearer throughout the process of minimizing. At the same time that minimalism frees up physical space in your home, it will free up "mind space" for you to reflect on and develop these purposes. Perhaps you would like to journal about your self-discoveries and come up with a written list of goals that you develop over time.

Most people, I find, have similar goals for their home. They want their home to take less time to care for and cost less money to maintain. They want less stress and distraction. They want more peace and space, more comfort and contentment.

But some people do have more individual desires for their home. For example, I have known artists who have wanted a decluttered home because they knew the change would help their creativity to expand. Some green-minded people I know are using minimalism to help them make less of a negative impact on the environment.

> A home that is filled with only the things you love and use will be a home that you love to use.
> #minimalisthome

After you've thought about your goals for your home, move on to your goals for your life as a whole.

I hope by now you're catching the vision that minimalism can give you a priceless gift of freedom that you can use to do greater things with your life. I'm not going to let you forget it, either! As thorough and practical as this book is about decluttering your home, it is about more than just decluttering. This is a book about reimagining what you can accomplish with your life.

Minimizing forces questions of values, meaning, and mission in life. Some initial de-owning and de-cluttering decisions are easy to make, but before long we realize that we're not sure what we want to keep until we know what we want to be doing with our time. And so minimalism becomes a lens through which we see the world and ourselves. We realize how consumeristic our society is, and we see how much we ourselves have been living according to that mind-set, focusing on earning and accumulation at the expense of loftier values. We wonder what we've been overlooking. Dreams both old and new begin to stir within our hearts.

The process of clarifying your life goals, however, won't be done when you finish minimizing your home. Goals can change with our seasons of life, fluctuating interests and passions, acquisition of new skills and credentials, people coming into and leaving our lives, and simple maturing and reflection. You'll be able to respond to changing conditions and make the most of new opportunities when you're not constrained by owning excess possessions.

Minimalism-enabled life goals can be of many types. They can include bucket-list items:

- traveling around the world
- running a marathon
- scuba diving in the Red Sea
- hiking the Appalachian Trail
- learning French and spending a summer in Paris

Minimalism-powered life goals can also include lifestyle changes:

- spending less time at work and more time with the kids
- losing weight and exercising regularly
- getting out of debt
- starting a part-time business
- moving into a low-maintenance condo that you can leave whenever the whim strikes

And then there's what I consider the most fulfilling goals of all—ones that help others.

In *The More of Less,* I tell the story about my wife and me starting a nonprofit with our minimalism dividend. Called The Hope Effect, it's an orphanage alternative that provides care for orphans in a way that mimics the family home. (Check it out at HopeEffect.com.) For orphans, too, there's no place like home, and I'm thankful to say The Hope Effect is now in operation in a growing number of countries. I can honestly say Kim and I couldn't be changing young lives in distant places if it hadn't been for minimizing our home. It's a purpose we never imagined when we started on this journey.

If you have the time and the means through minimizing, there are so many ways, both big and small, to help others:

- teaching English to refugees
- creating and managing a donor-advised fund
- taking that gap year you never had and serving a nonprofit overseas

- adopting a child
- volunteering at the same donation center where you're going to be taking a bunch of your unneeded stuff

I just know that something inside you yearns to accomplish memorable objectives, live in a way that is more fulfilling to you, and make the world a better place with the overflow of your gifts and time. You bring it all within reach when you move past your "stuff problem."

If you've been feeling frustrated about your house, most likely much of the reason lies here—in a lack of alignment between your possessions and your purposes. You've got stuff that's distracting you. Stuff that's taking up your time. Stuff that's absorbing resources you could better use elsewhere. You're bound by your house instead of freed by it. So do something about it! Get rid of all those things that aren't helping you and pursue your purposes with greater passion and freedom.

But look, don't let this get too heavy. You don't have to agonize over the meaning of your life every time you are trying to decide whether to keep a spatula or a pair of socks. Sometimes items do have a direct impact on a person's future, such as a reminder of a past relationship that is keeping someone from moving on. But other times, the impact of items is more indirect. We just have too much stuff. We need to get down to what's really valuable to us to clear the runway for what we can do with the rest of our lives.

We remove the clutter from our home to better live the life we desire. And if we're living with a spouse and other family members, they deserve better lives too.

The Conversations You Need to Have

I still laugh about the first conversation I had with my mother in which I told her I was planning to become a minimalist.

"Oh, Joshua," she said, "I was just watching *Oprah* and she was interviewing some minimalists. Did you know that they don't go to the grocery store, but they get their food out of dumpsters?"

Obviously there are some misconceptions about minimalism out there. Not everybody knows as much about minimalism or is at the same point of coming on board with minimalism as you are. And so if your intention is to minimize your entire house and you live with others, then it's important that you discuss the value of decluttering and work together with the other members of your household to accomplish it.

I recommend you call a family meeting. (You might need more than one. That's okay.) Explain in positive terms what minimalism is—*the removing of unnecessary possessions so we can better live the life we want as a family.* Talk about why you want a minimalist home, what the minimalism makeover process might look like, and what benefits you're hoping to get out of it. Brainstorm places where you could donate your unneeded items. Invite questions and comments. Maybe you'll want to make it a walking meeting, strolling through the house with your family to look at the clutter and begin imagining what the rooms will look like after you take out all the excess.

The purpose here is not to criticize anyone about the clutter in the home. It's to start talking in positive terms about the upcoming process. And it's to share the vision of minimalism and help all your family members glimpse the beauty of what could be. Do it well, and this just might be a major turning point, with consequences reverberating for generations to come. Honestly, this process could be revolutionary for you and your entire family!

If you're married, the most important person to have on your side is your spouse. Disagreements with your spouse over specific choices about what you will remove from the home may be inevitable. But at the outset, if you can agree in principle with him or her about the project of minimizing your home, you will have all but ensured the eventual success of your minimalism home makeover.

In this conversation with your spouse, you will find out what he thinks about minimalism and discover what barriers you might encounter. Don't expect instant or perfect agreement about minimalism. The two of you should take as much time as necessary to picture a new minimalist lifestyle as equal partners. Encourage your spouse to read this book and discuss it with you.

After you've been through all this, if your partner still *really* doesn't want to minimize, don't get mad. Don't get manipulative. Certainly, don't wait until your partner is out of the house and then start throwing out her stuff! Honor the fact that she needs more time to digest this new approach to material ownership. It could be that the prospect of minimizing is causing your spouse to deal with some inner turmoil of some sort, such as emotional baggage from the past or toxic self-criticism. Don't harm the relationship by trying to force minimalism on your loved one.

Inspiration

KID CONVERTS

The kids have all reacted differently to my vigorous removal of stuff we don't need.

My seventeen-year-old son was nervous about the idea—I think he thought we might drag them off to live in a cave or something. But he's slowly getting the idea more and more.

My fifteen-year-old daughter loves to keep every trinket and piece of paper she has ever owned and loves to get new things whenever she can. Every nook and cranny was overflowing. This process has been more difficult for her, but she is feeling the benefits—even if she can't articulate them quite yet. She is seeing a positive change in our home. For now, she has a self-imposed fifty items of clothing limit and has removed a lot of the storage spaces so she can't cram much in. It's definitely been toughest for her.

My five-year-old boy, among all three kids, took to the idea most

As you are waiting for your mate to fully come around to the idea of a minimalist makeover for your shared home, you can start by minimizing your own clothes and other personal possessions. In addition, perhaps your partner would not mind your minimizing certain parts of the house on your own, if you'll agree to leave other parts untouched for the time being. Based on my observation of many couples in this kind of situation, I can say that very likely your example will open your partner's eyes to the benefits of owning less and cause him to want to join the decluttering crusade. Waiting for this outcome can tax your patience, but if the relationship is preserved and your partner eventually becomes your ally in minimalism, it will be worth it.

When it comes to enlisting kids in your minimalism makeover, a lot depends on their ages. The basic principle is that the older the child, the less

---

excitedly. After some months of observing what we were doing, at my prompting, he went through his toys and chose which things he could give to someone who needed it more. He actually discarded about two-thirds of his things—far more than we ever imagined he'd choose to minimize right away.

Minimizing with a family is not always easy. But it's important. Our kids are always watching and always learning from us. And while I don't notice the progress each day, I know it's happening.

We just came back from a holiday in which we stayed in two different people's homes. Anytime the kids opened a drawer or cupboard and noticed a cluttered mess inside, they expressed their gratitude for the changes we have been making at home with statements like "I can't believe we used to live like this." That trip reminded me why this is so important.

—Glenda, Australia

directive you should be about what needs to go. Just as with your spouse, don't create resentment by trying to force minimalism on older elementary or teenage children. Keep explaining, keep encouraging, and keep modeling minimalism. Negotiate ownership limits and boundaries in ways that make sense to them. Remember, this is a chance to convey a new value of simplicity to your kids that can benefit them for the rest of their lives, so approach this as a chance to help them grow.

In my book *Clutterfree with Kids,* I ask how we can help our kids break free from the world's drive to consume. Then I say,

> We come to a point where we realize there is more to life than what the
> world is peddling. We admit we have foolishly bought what the world
> is selling—and our lives are still empty. Possessions have not bought
> happiness. Money has not provided security. Popularity and power
> have not satisfied. . . . The answers clearly do not lie in a life conformed
> to the unoriginal culture of our day. We know it to be true. And we
> seek desperately for teachable moments to transfer this understanding
> to our kids.[1]

This is big stuff. There may be few better things you can do for your kids than teach them minimalism.

Once you have the kids in agreement with you about the desire to declutter (even if they're still somewhat wary about what this will mean), enlist their help in sorting and removing excess possessions throughout the house. If they're old enough, let them take the lead in their own rooms. You'll definitely want their help in the future in maintaining your home's minimalism by not bringing too much into the house and by doing their share in keeping the house tidy. They'll be pleased to know that minimalism is going to make their chores around the house easier because there will be less to take care of.

Becoming minimalist is hard, whether it's you, your spouse, or your kids doing it. So when the members of your family start helping out with decluttering your home, don't take it lightly. Be generous with your thanks, and try to get your whole family to encourage one another to keep it up. Share with the others both the work of minimizing and the rewards that come from it.

From Easier to Harder

Alongside the members of your family, you're undertaking the creation of a minimalist home, not a *part* of a minimalist home. You'll get the full benefits of living with less—and be more likely to keep them—if you minimize every room in your home. But that raises the question of what order you should follow when attacking the rooms in your home.

It's your home. You can minimize your rooms in whatever sequence you like. But if you want to give yourself the best chance of home minimizing success, then there is only one approach I would recommend to you. I call it *easier to harder*. You start with rooms that are comparatively easy to minimize and then move on to harder ones. Working in the easier rooms builds up your skill and confidence in minimizing as you go. And since the easier rooms also tend to be the most lived-in rooms, you and your family get to experience a lot of benefit from your work quickly. You minimize each space entirely before going on to the next. And you don't stop until you're done with the entire house.

The order of the next eight chapters reveals what I mean by *easier to harder*. Approach the spaces in your home this way:

First, your living room and family room.

Second, your own bedroom and the other bedrooms in the house.

Third, all the clothes closets.

Fourth, your home's bathrooms and the laundry room.

Fifth, your kitchen and dining areas.

Sixth, your home office.

Seventh, your storage areas, including your toy room and craft work spaces.

Eighth, your garage and yard.

You may not have all these spaces in your home. You might even have some spaces that are not mentioned here. But this list covers all the spaces most homes are likely to have, and for most people this represents the easier-to-harder progression. Plan your minimizing schedule in this order.

By the way, if you want to quickly find the step-by-step instructions for minimizing any particular type of space, look for the star (★) indicating that section of the chapter.

Do I Need This?

As you go room by room decluttering your home, you'll have to face all the possessions you've accumulated over the years and decide what to keep and what to discard. I encourage you to handle every item. Don't just look at an item; take it in your hand and think about why you got it in the first place, what it does for you, and whether it should stay in the home any longer. What it will come down to is this simple question: *Do I need this?*

If you do need it, you should keep it—and that's fine. If you don't need it, then it can go—and that's fine too.

In psychological theory, the *endowment effect* is our tendency to consider an object more important than it really is simply because we own it. This explains why it's so hard for us to get rid of our stuff. It's *ours!* Reflexively, we want to hold on to it. And so we have to deliberately disendow our possessions of the false value we have assigned them. The question *Do I need this?* helps us cut through the irrationalism of our excess accumulation.

Of course, our human needs are actually quite slim: water, food, shelter, and clothing. But it's important to note we're talking about more than mere survival here. What we're talking about is realizing our fullest potential. It's about the pursuit of high-level goals. So when we ask, *Do I need this?* we're actually asking, *Does this help me achieve my purpose or hinder me in that pursuit?* This is a robust framework that allows us to make decisions about what to keep and what to remove.

Remember that, to be necessary for our personal potential, an object doesn't always have to be strictly utilitarian, such as a can opener you need because you're going to have cans to open.

Beauty is necessary to the human condition too. Maybe you have a unique glass vase that you bought at a gallery. You don't need it for survival, but it delights your senses and provides inspiration and optimism every time you look at it with the sun streaming through it. In a sense, your soul needs it to be healthy and complete. From that perspective, you would be well advised to get rid of some other decorative objects in that room, thereby giving greater prominence to this one.

Similarly, you may wish to keep something because it has overwhelming value as a memento. If you inherited your grandparents' wedding photo and it inspires fond remembrances of them, keep it. I don't recommend you hold on to every keepsake or inherited item that has come into your possession, but you can keep the most meaningful of them. Even as you get rid of objects that are weighing you down, put these most special objects out where you will see them often. In this way, minimalism can actually help you keep connections with past generations more effectively than hoarding ever could.

For something to be necessary and help you fulfill your purpose and potential, it needs to be so useful, lovely, or meaningful that you must keep it. Some objects will meet those criteria. Many others will not. The reality is, in our overcrowded homes today, most possessions are not truly "belongings"— they don't really belong in our houses anymore. They are only distracting us from the things that do belong. You're going to have to make a decision about object after object as you go through your house to minimize it. So get ready.

Understand, however, that your decisions many times will not be simple ones—an object either has value for you or it does not. Whatever combination of function, aesthetics, and sentiment an object in your home might represent, there can be arguments on both sides of the question of whether to keep it or get rid of it. Something might *sort of* help you in living a purposeful life and yet might also *sort of* hinder you. Instead of an obvious yes or no, it might be more like weighing the alternatives on a scale.

Never organize what you can discard.
#minimalisthome

The way I think of it is that, in addition to whatever monetary price an object may originally have had, it also has an ongoing "clutter cost" in terms of the money, time, energy, and space it demands from you. That "clutter cost" may or may not be greater than its present value for you in terms of its utility, beauty, or meaning. Or in other words, an object is both a *burden* and a *benefit*—at the same time. So you're going to have to weigh both sides and make a benefit-versus-burden judgment call.

If you're honest about the relative weights of the benefits you get from your possessions and the burdens they place on you, I believe you'll decide that many of your possessions really aren't worth holding on to. Ask yourself, *Do I need this? Really* need it? Not if its burden is greater than its benefit.

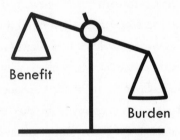

The well-known Pareto Principle (named after an economist) says that in many situations around 80 percent of the effects come from around 20 percent of the causes. As applied to our homes, this principle suggests that we might use 20 percent of our possessions around 80 percent of the time. This doesn't necessarily mean you can get rid of 80 percent of the possessions in your home (though I've known people who have done that—and more), but it does suggest that when you use necessity as the basis for deciding what to keep, you're going to be able to get rid of *a lot*.

Go into your minimalist home makeover picturing yourself not getting rid of a little here and there but eliminating large quantities and even whole categories of possessions. Why not, if they're not necessary?

A Self-Energizing Process

When I started minimizing our home back in 2008, it didn't take long for me to begin recognizing significant ways my life was improving.

Only two days into minimalism, the first benefit occurred to me. As I was getting rid of things—and had no intention of replacing them with new things—I realized that owning less offered a financial opportunity. As we accumulated fewer things, we would spend less money. Additionally, it would cost much less because we would have fewer things to store, maintain, repair, and clean.

Just one day later it occurred to me how my new life would be affecting my kids. My son was five and my daughter two, and they were both soaking up values from us as parents about how to live and how to achieve significance. Becoming minimalist modeled for my children the beliefs that personal belongings are not the key to happiness, that security is found in character, and that the pursuit of happiness runs on a different road than the pursuit of possessions.

The next day—less than ninety-six hours into pursuing minimalism—I noticed how it was becoming easier to find things in my house.

Over the coming days and months, I noticed how easy it was becoming to clean the house . . . how the process was freeing me from past mistakes . . . how my home and life were becoming more peaceful and less stressful . . . and how minimalism was allowing me to own higher-quality things.

Here's the point of all this: those benefits kept me going! The more I noticed and was able to articulate how owning less was improving my life in practical ways, the more I wanted it. What started as a simple feeling of calm sitting in a newly minimized living room or decluttered vehicle provided motivation to move forward.

A MINIMIZING ACCELERATOR: REMOVING DUPLICATES

When I was just getting started on my minimalist journey, I ran across an article in which the writer said you need only two towels—one in use and one in the laundry. I remember thinking, *Huh, I guess she has a point.*

I opened my linen closet and noticed at least twenty towels. There were new towels in the front, old towels in the back, even some animal-shaped towels for the kids. And that didn't include the towels in the guest bathroom downstairs, or the hand towels and washcloths, or the beach towels in that other closet.

Now, we were a family of four. So obviously we'd need more than two towels total. But the ideal number was certainly less than we had. So we got rid of quite a few. We just didn't *need* as many as we had.

More importantly, I began noticing duplicates everywhere: televisions, pillows, blankets, jeans, shoes, coats, cleaning supplies, brushes, coffee mugs, Tupperware, pots and pans, staplers, scissors, games, tools. . . . In all these categories, we had accumulated unnecessary multiples, so removing the extras was an easy way to start minimizing all around our home.

If you're looking to make progress in whatever room you enter to minimize, identify the duplicates. Keep your favorite, or maybe a few favorites, in each category. Get rid of the rest. It will be a good way to make progress—fast.

There is no doubt you will quickly begin to see the positive results of owning fewer possessions as soon as your first room is completed. Pay attention to these advantages as they come. Reflect on them. Savor them. Discuss them with the others in your family. In this way, the process of minimizing will itself energize you to keep going until you have reached your goal of a fully decluttered house.

We minimize not out of guilt but because of our goals. It's a positive process. Let's enjoy it and make the most of it.

And then as we near the end, let's see how the process has caused us to rethink and expand our goals for what we can do with the rest of our lives. Our home minimalism makeover becomes a makeover of us when we let it transform our future.

Friend of the Poor

Anya is a nurse, wife, and mother who decluttered her home in Hawaii. She loves how her family's home has become much more open and easy to maintain. But more came out of her minimalism home makeover than just that benefit. She wrote to me, "Realizing that my time does not need to be spent on possessions has been liberating. I noticed that once I had more time available, I had to define what my life passions were."

Just to be clear, minimalism doesn't *guarantee* you find more meaning and significance in life. But it does, almost always, open your eyes wider to these issues and create a context where you can think through them better. That's what happened to Anya, and she was determined to get it right.

"As I let go of my possessions," Anya said, "I was much more inclined to share my time and finances with others. By spending less on possessions, I was able to decrease my hours at work. Once I stepped back from that environment, I was able to think, *What type of nursing would I do if my hourly wage did not matter?*"

For Anya, this meant the reawakening of a dormant dream.

Over the years, she had thought about how rewarding it would be to use her nursing skills to care for underserved populations in foreign countries. But each time, the thought had faded. She had her job, first with the US military and then with a private medical practice. She had bills to pay and things to take care of at home. And so the longing to serve the poor remained unfulfilled, leaving a vague sense of dissatisfaction in her heart.

All that changed as a result of the mental refocusing that minimizing brought with it.

In the summer of 2017, Anya joined a team to provide medical care to poor families in Honduras through the nonprofit Friends of Barnabas. During that volunteer trip, she traveled to five different communities with a mobile clinic. Her team saw everything from common colds to cardiac anomalies, hypertension, and hypoglycemia. They treated more than a thousand patients, referring the most serious and surgical cases to a facility equipped to take care of them. She loved the warm, smiling welcome she received from the Hondurans, and at the same time she felt her own heart expanding.

She came back from Honduras a different person. "When I got home, I hugged my husband and son tighter," she said. "On top of that, I saw the homeless man on the street who needed ice water and food on a ninety-eight-degree day with new eyes. I didn't stress about the ten minutes needed to provide for him and tell him he was cared about."

Today, Anya is planning more trips where she can volunteer her medical skills for the poor. And she recommends minimizing to anyone who wants better relationships and a more meaningful life. "Removing the excess allows time and focus that we need to make a loving connection to those around us," she related. "You don't have to go to another country or have medical training to enjoy the benefits of minimalism. It can start right in your family and community. However, if you feel pulled toward other countries and cultures, not being tied down and attached to belongings allows you the opportunities to explore and serve freely."

I don't know what dream is bubbling within your mind. Or maybe you don't have a dream right now—but one day you will. Minimalism will unearth a hidden passion in you even as it unearths the home that your house ought to be. But whatever motivates you, consider minimalism the step you need to take to remove the barriers to pursuing major life goals. Sure, making the decision to minimize requires you to overcome inertia, tendencies, and stagnation, but the momentum that comes from it can carry you to a whole new and better place in life.

NOT SURE? EXPERIMENT!

Sometimes it's easy to know when it's time to get rid of something in your home. Other times, not so much.

The electric skillet—needed or not?

Those blue pumps that you like but that are similar to the black pair—needed or not?

The gas-powered blower you bought to scatter leaves in the fall—needed or not?

To help you make the harder choices in de-owning, or the ones that you and another member of your household disagree over, try doing without an item for a set period of time. I often recommend twenty-nine days. Only afterward decide whether it's necessary to your home or superfluous. I call this *experimenting*.

After your trial period, if you find yourself wishing you had the item because it would have come in handy or you otherwise missed it, then maybe you should keep it. On the other hand, if you find yourself getting along without it just fine, then go ahead and get rid of it. Either way—experiment successful! Now you know.

You Can Do It!

Now that you've seen how minimizing can transform your home and your life, I hope you're raring to go and can hardly wait to turn to the next chapter and get started. But then again, you *might* still be hesitant. So let's touch on one more important point before we jump into our first space. Maybe you don't need a vision to help you stick to the trail until you get to the summit—maybe you need a shove to get you started on the hike in the first place! If so, these thoughts are for you.

Over the years, I've heard just about every reason why someone feels held back from minimizing his or her home:

- "I've always been a messy person. I can't change now."
- "This house is too big, and we've been collecting stuff for too long. We'll never be able to get through it all."
- "Between my job and my husband and the kids and getting to Pilates twice a week, I don't have time for something else."
- "We've got a major crisis going on in the family, and that's taking up all our attention right now."
- "I tried decluttering before and didn't get very far. Why should it be different this time?"

I don't consider these to be excuses, at least not usually. There's some truth in all these statements, and they often reflect serious human pain. But I also know that it's possible to go ahead and minimize a home despite issues like these. Why? Because I've seen it done so many times.

Heather: "After my seventh baby joined our family, in the midst of postpartum depression and feeling like I couldn't keep up with everything asked of me, my life felt completely out of control. I cleaned up the same messes every day and never actually decluttered anything. My house felt the opposite of peaceful. But then I heard about minimalism. It has changed my house, health, and relationships. I've lost thirty pounds, taken control of my house, and have more time for my family."

Mayda: "I am a retired teacher of thirty-four years and a hoarder because of my environment. From the time I was little, my dad always said, 'Don't pollute Grandmother Earth' and 'Waste not, want not,' so a desire to hold on to things became my driving attitude. With all that and thirty-four years of teaching materials, the stuff has definitely piled up! I'm on the path to minimalism by changing my lifelong attitude of needing to save everything."

Ali: "I'm a second-time divorced mom of two—one severely autistic— and I have an autoimmune illness and terrible anxiety. I was forced to sell our house and a car. Despite fear, fatigue, and panic attacks, I uncluttered years of stuff. My kids and I got rid of 80 percent of our belongings. It was tough and exhausting, but going through that was better than not. We learned a new way of living—it was such a relief. Months later, when we moved into an eight-hundred-square-foot apartment, we decided to declutter more and more. I never thought I would enjoy living with less or that it was possible, but it became true for us. It is possible for anyone!"

If there is one secret formula to living simply and clutter-free, it is this: *believe it is possible and take the next step.* Do that, and you'll bring the mountain peak within reach.

Of course the path to being clutter-free will take some time, but imposing a demanding deadline on yourself is *not* part of the Becker Method. I believe it's a good thing to make steady progress and keep up the momentum so you don't stall out, but there's no one looking over your shoulder to make sure you finish your home makeover by a certain date. Conquer the project room by room on your own schedule, and eventually you'll be done. The completion will be wonderful whenever it occurs.

Not every possession is a belonging.
#minimalisthome

You *can* conquer your clutter. Believe it. Mind over mess!

Next, we're going to get into the specific spaces of your home. When you're ready to read the next chapter, have a seat in your living room—because that's the room you're going to be minimizing first.

Action recommendation: *As you're minimizing your home space by space, take before-and-after pictures or videos and share your progress with your friends over social media (use #minimalisthome). The positive responses you get from them will encourage you to keep going, and—who knows?—you might motivate some of them to start their own minimalism home makeover.*

PART 2

Spaces

3

"Us" Rooms

Decluttering the Living Room and Family Room

I was standing outside my garage the first time I heard the word *minimalism,* and not being one to hesitate when I know I'm on to something good, I undertook my first decluttering project right then and there—the car parked in front of me. I found this task easy enough. While there was plenty of stuff piled up on the seats, on the floors, and in the glove compartment, there weren't a lot of hard decisions to make. I knew I didn't need that CD anymore, or that map, or those Happy Meal toys. So I finished in short order.

Quickly, I moved on to the living room, mostly because I knew it was another space I could find success in. My living room was full of things that didn't pass the *Do I need this?* test—a pile of magazines, rows of DVDs, odds and ends that had collected on the side tables, shelves of decorations that held no particular meaning, and toys piled in a corner. Still, it wasn't the most crowded place in the house, not like our jam-packed kitchen drawers or our scary closets with their looming boxes, for instance. Although clearing out our living room required more time and energy than sifting through the contents of a Toyota Corolla, it was still a project I could complete in a matter of hours. And that's what I did.

Immediately afterward, I sat my tired self down on the couch in the living room that I had just minimized (at least for my first time through) and looked around at what I had accomplished. I remember the moment distinctly because it was an odd experience viewing my "new" living room. With fewer physical possessions obstructing my view or demanding my attention, everything felt calmer, more peaceful. It had been a lot of work, but it was worth it. I commented to my wife, "It almost feels like energy is able to move more freely in this space with fewer things cluttering the area."

It was a feeling that would motivate me to create a similar atmosphere in my bedroom, my bathroom, my office, and all around the house. This important victory provided me with confidence and motivation going forward.

In this chapter, we're going to start giving you a minimalist home makeover in two manageable areas: your living room and its more laid-back cousin, your family room (if you have one). I know that, from home to home, the time required to minimize these rooms may vary significantly, but for most people, minimizing the living room and family room represents an accomplishable goal. If you begin here, you'll score a win relatively quickly, *and* you'll start building up your mental and emotional "muscles" for decluttering.

If you happen to be one of those people who have a living room or family room where *everything* seems to collect (I see that a lot in small apartments), never fear. What you'll learn in this chapter will help you tackle these rooms bit by bit until it's all done. The living room and family room are still great places for you to get started in creating the home and life you want. And if you've got mountains of possessions in those rooms . . . well, your victory over them will be all the sweeter for you. You'll get a lot done—and in an important place.

When you think about it, the living and family rooms are the most public places in your private home, aren't they? Here is where you can get together with all the loved ones you live with. Here is where you invite your friends to sit down with you and talk, or have tea, or watch the Super Bowl on television. If you host a club or a church or neighborhood group, it's likely you'll be gathering in one of these rooms. These are your "us" rooms. So minimizing in these rooms immediately starts helping you not only to enjoy the benefits of minimizing yourself but also to share them with others.

Relationships are the "life" of the "body" that is a home. You can start enhancing those relationships at once by beginning your minimalism makeover in the prime gathering places of your home: the living room and family room.

WHAT TO DO WITH THE THINGS YOU REMOVE

1. Donate

Salvation Army, Goodwill, and similar nonprofits will take your unwanted belongings and resell them at a low price to people who can't afford new things. Or maybe you have a locally based nonprofit (homeless shelter, refugee resettlement program, battered women's clinic, or whatever it may be) that accepts donations. You'll feel good helping them out. And you'll get a tax deduction too.

2. Sell

Garage sales and online sales are possibilities for some unwanted items that maintain value. Just have a realistic understanding of how long it might take to sell them and how much you might get for them so that you're not disappointed. If you find yourself selling items for a fraction of their original cost, don't get depressed because of it. Use the experience as a reminder of how it's so often better not to buy something in the first place.

3. Throw away or recycle

If something is no good to you anymore and nobody else is going to want it, then decide whether it goes in the trash bin or the recycling bin. Please recycle whenever you can. Minimalism isn't just for our own benefit; it is also a practice that is kind to the environment and to future generations.

What You Want Out of Your
Public-Private Spaces

A living room is a space that almost every home has. Two-thirds of newly built homes in the United States also have a separate family room. In a throwback to earlier days, more and more homes today have a "great room" combining the functions of a living room and family room.[1] If the floor plan is open concept, such spaces may flow into other rooms, usually a kitchen or dining room. But regardless of how it does it, every home tries to accommodate human gathering.

If you have a separate living room, it is probably the most formal place in your house, prepared as a space not only where the members of your household

---

Inspiration

THE GATHERING SPACE

The great room in our home was often wasted space. We wanted it to be just the opposite. We wanted the room to be an area where people—both in our family and from outside our family—would feel comfortable to stop, sit, relax, and chat.

We minimized this room with dinner parties and gatherings with friends and family in mind. As a result, we kept a table and chairs, placed two vintage chairs by the fireplace, and hung our daughters' artwork on the wall. No TV. It was all about conversation. My husband even began referring to the room as "the gathering space" to further promote the goal we had in mind.

And wouldn't you know it? Once we began crafting that room around a specific purpose, the room began to serve it.

There was one moment I will never forget shortly after we finished this room. Two of our daughters returned home after a particularly

can get together but also where you can entertain guests and feel proud about the surroundings. You might put your finest furniture here, mount your most attractive artwork on the wall, and take your best shot at decorating tastefully. You've probably got the seating arranged in a pattern conducive to conversation. Maybe you've placed interesting objects on shelves to serve as conversation starters.

If you have a separate family room, it is similar in a lot of ways to your living room but may be more casual and comfortable. Although you could invite your guests to sit down here, this is first of all the place where the members of the household go when they want to get together. Here you've paid attention to making sure the couches and chairs are comfortable, and you may have set up the seating for easy television viewing. Maybe you have family photos on the

---

difficult evening. Just steps inside the door, exhausted, they both plopped down in those vintage chairs and started talking. My husband and I exchanged a glance, and what would have, in a typical living or family room, been a few minutes of chatter followed by drowning in any number of distractions turned into the first significant moment in that space. We pulled out pencils and paper and brainstormed ideas about how to handle their situation.

Over the years, this simple, decluttered area by the fireplace in our great room has become the most sacred spot in our home. If anyone needs anything, she knows that if she takes a seat, someone will be along any second to chat, play, cry, plan, or whatever. I truly believe the simplicity of the space is what contributes to its sanctity. The removal of the unnecessary has allowed the most important things to take precedence.

—Jessica, USA

wall, reminding you of loved ones and the happy times you've spent together. Maybe this is where you keep games, puzzles, and other diversions to share.

Now, this is my point in going into all this: Just as you should have purposes in mind for *your home as a whole,* so you should have purposes in mind for *each room in your home,* including the living and family rooms. As you're minimizing in a methodical way, you should bear in mind these room purposes so you can decide whether the possessions within them belong there or not. Whenever something in a room doesn't further your goals for it, then it is a candidate for removal. The purposeful leads right into the practical.

For example, maybe you will decide that your living room, as it stands today, is too formal. It's not a comfortable place and rarely gets used. So maybe you will start minimizing by getting rid of items that make it feel too stuffy. Maybe you realize you don't really need seating for ten in your living room; you never have that many people over at one time anyway. Get rid of a sofa, and all of a sudden your conversation grouping is more intimate.

Maybe you have a recliner where you love to sit in the family room. Park yourself there and look around, asking yourself which objects enhance the peacefulness of that setting for you and which do not.

Maybe you need to eliminate a bunch of toys your kids have outgrown so they have room to play with the ones they still like.

Maybe you don't like how much time you and your family members are spending on electronic devices. In that case it could be time to get rid of a television set or game console.

Since these rooms are places used by the whole household, of course you should also ask the members of your family what they would like to keep or get rid of in these rooms. Talk out your minimizing strategies in these rooms *together.* Do the work of removing items *together.* Enjoy the benefits *together.* This is the perfect way to establish your minimalism home makeover as a family project, with buy-in and celebration all around.

If you live alone, you might want to ask a close friend to come over and give you some advice about what to hold on to or eliminate, from the perspective of someone who frequents your home as a guest. She'll be glad to give her opinion. And besides, you might need help moving furniture!

Put your work clothes on. Get some boxes ready. It's time to get started transforming your home.

THE CONVENIENCE FALLACY

There are certain places in our homes where we tend to leave items out because we think it will make it easier for us to grab them when we want them. I'm talking about things like these:

- old DVDs of our favorite movies piled on the entertainment center
- small appliances occupying space on our kitchen counters
- toiletries clustered beside our bathroom sinks
- office supplies on our home-office desktop
- tools on our tool benches

By leaving these things out, we think we're saving time when we need them. We think we're simplifying our lives.

I call this the convenience fallacy.

Consider those old CDs you've held on to for years in a CD tower in your family room. Sure, by leaving them out, you save a couple of seconds when you want to grab one of them. But for the other 99.9 percent of the time, they're sitting out where they create visual distraction. Since it would take very little time to pull a CD out of a storage cabinet and put it back when you're done, wouldn't it be better to keep it out of sight instead of where it's contributing to clutter and acting as nothing more than a visual distraction in your space?

The same goes for most, if not all, of the things we leave out for "convenience" around the house.

★ STEP-BY-STEP MINIMIZING FOR YOUR LIVING ROOM AND FAMILY ROOM

As you're working through these stages and handling each object, remember to ask yourself, *Does this align with my purposes? Is it so useful that I have to keep it, so beautiful that I can't live without it, or so personally meaningful that it has to stay with me?* In other words, *Do I need this?* Whenever the answer is no, get rid of an item, and do it gladly. The space you open up will be more worthwhile to you than whatever you're removing.

1. Relocate Things That Don't Belong

In a minimalist home, every item has its own "home." Some things "live" in the garage; others "live" in the basement, the bedroom closet, or a drawer in the kitchen. When your house is overcrowded, finding "homes" for every item can be difficult, but the more you minimize, the easier you'll find this to be.

So as you approach your living room or family room, begin by relocating those things that don't belong there, returning them to the room(s) where they should be. For example, maybe dishes need to go back to the kitchen. Or some tools left in the corner need to go back out to the garage.

I know this isn't minimizing. It's rearranging. But it's also a precursor to minimizing because sometimes it's easier to decide what to keep and what to eliminate when you see an entire category of possessions in one place.

On the other hand, if you do pick up some things that don't belong in the living room or family room and realize immediately that you don't need them at all, don't wait to minimize them. Go ahead and place them in a box for discarding or donating, and get them out of your home altogether.

The momentum is just getting started!

2. Clear the Flat Surfaces

Next, begin to tackle open, flat spaces, by which I mean shelves, bookcases, tabletops, and the like.

It's interesting to me how so many of us accumulate the same sorts of items on these surfaces. Vases. Candles. Souvenirs. Ornaments. Propped-up photos. Art books. Collections of figurines. Individually, there may be nothing wrong with any of these items. Collectively, they can become too much. How quickly they begin to distract attention and clutter up a room!

Don't let that trend continue in your home. Remove the knickknacks and decorations that no longer serve you. If a target number is helpful, try to remove 50 percent.

Keeping just the items that mean the most to you will help them get noticed. (More on this soon.)

3. Declutter the Entertainment Center

Move on to the entertainment center, if you have one. These large pieces of furniture often harbor lots of small items that we don't need anymore. They can look messy and be a pain to search through when we're looking for something we want (usually in a hurry). So do something about yours now.

Take out old electronic components, cords you don't need, and discs and games that nobody is going to use anymore. Get rid of them. (Please recycle electronics responsibly. Check the guidelines for your area.) And then arrange the devices you do use in an eye-pleasing display, hiding their cords as much as possible.

You may have DVDs, CDs, and pieces of video game hardware that are often left out to make them easy to grab. Change that thinking. Rather than leaving anything in plain view, put those items in the freed-up hidden spaces you are about to create in the next step. The more we leave out where we can see it, the more of a distraction and source of stress it becomes.

4. Dig In to Storage Areas in These Rooms

Some of the best spots for drastic minimizing in the living and family rooms are spaces that are hidden from sight: cabinets, drawers, game closet, and so on. A room might look neat when these spaces are shut off from view, but *you* know how much stuff is packed in there. And you're the one who is going to be wasting time whenever you try to dig stuff out of these crowded places. So be ruthless in removing items from there.

Decks of cards, packs of matches, old magazines, out-of-season decorations, dog-eared books, throw blankets—these are just a few of the things we tend to keep hidden away in the living or family room because we "might want them." But will we really? For many people, the items stored in places that are hidden from view have not been needed for years. You may not remember where yours came from or why you got them in the first place. Free up that space by removing everything you don't need. You'll want to use the space for things that are actually worth keeping.

5. Remove Furniture and Other Large Items

After you've removed the smaller things from the room, you should have a better sense of whether some larger pieces in the room might be no longer necessary and are just in the way. What larger items have you got in your living room or family room? A big fake plant? An ottoman you trip over like Dick Van Dyke? A display hutch you inherited from Grandma but never really liked? A high-back chair hardly anyone sits on because it's so uncomfortable? A set of pillows everyone just keeps moving back and forth on the couch?

Depending on how large the item is, you might need a plan for getting rid of it, such as scheduling a truck to come and pick up a piece of furniture for a donation site. That's okay. As soon as you can, get it outta there! See what a big difference it makes immediately.

Things That Tell Your Story

As you look around the living and family rooms, ask yourself, *What culture am I establishing in these places? What am I communicating to my family and friends?*

Minimalist Home Value

TOGETHERNESS

Would you like some good news for a change? Parents are spending more time with their kids.

Believe it or not, it's true. A University of California study showed that moms, on average, spent nearly twice as much time with their kids in 2012 compared to moms in 1965 (104 minutes daily in 2012 versus 54 minutes daily in 1965). Meanwhile, the time that dads are spending with their kids has nearly quadrupled—an average of 59 minutes a day in 2012, compared to an average of 16 minutes in 1965.[2] I love it!

Don't you agree this is a trend we should keep pushing along?

That's one reason why it's so important for us to make sure that those parts of our homes where people gather have an inviting aspect, are functioning well, and aren't requiring us to spend more time taking care of our stuff than interacting with the people we care about. The kitchen and eating spaces are prime places where people get together in our homes, but even more deliberately, the family room and living room are designed to bring people together. And it's not just bringing together parents with kids, by the way, but kids with kids and Mom with Dad too. In fact, anyone who happens to live in the household, plus the guests who come over, will gather in these spaces.

To know we are loved and understood, we have to spend time together with our loved ones, intergenerationally talking and enjoying shared activities—the kinds of things, in other words, that take place so well in a peaceful, clutter-free living or family room.

Two of the primary ways that those rooms speak to those who occupy them are with the items we put out for display and the photos or artwork we put up on the wall.

Display Items on Shelves

I have a friend with a bookcase in her living room. The last time I visited her, I noticed the following on its four shelves: thirty-six books, eleven figurines, twenty-four photos, two souvenir coffee mugs, ten snow globes (and it wasn't even winter), various flower arrangements in vases, and a small sampling of candles. Yes, I actually wrote down the inventory . . . when she wasn't noticing.

As I looked at her bookcase, I asked myself, *Which of these things mean the most to her? What is it that she values most?* I couldn't tell by looking at her bookcase—it was too crowded with things that were *un*important.

One benefit of minimalism is that you are able to visibly declare what is important to you. Look around your living room and family room again. What do the remaining items communicate? If a stranger walked in, what would he identify as most important to you? *Is* it most important? Or have the most important things in your life become crowded out by less significant things?

What would your family say your living room, family room, or great room communicates about your values? Do your decorations tell a story? Do they communicate a culture? What about the layout of the furniture? Does it promote family interaction or simply focus all eyes on the television? Is that what you want?

Pictures on Walls

A few years ago, we decided we wanted our home to better share our story. Our desire was to decorate in a way that clearly communicated what was most important to us as a family.

As a result, we removed outdated objects, knickknacks collecting dust, and any decoration bought only because it matched the color of our couch.

What remained were the pieces most important to us: photos of our family and growing children, a scenic image of Vermont given to us by friends, a beautiful piece of art we received on our wedding day, and a few items that have always been important to my wife. Each of our decorations tells a story. Our home and the pictures on our walls display what is most important to us.

Now, I realize that personal tastes in this matter vary widely. The art of making a home is always going to look different from person to person. And I know we hang far fewer pictures on our walls than most.

But generally speaking, we all tend to hang the same types of pictures on our walls: We hang photos of our family. We mount photos from places we have visited or would like to visit. We put up inspirational words about love and laughter and living life to the fullest. We frame images of a life filled with quietness and rest.

Ask yourself what is really important and then have the courage to build your home and life around that answer. #minimalisthome

---

Nobody hangs images on their walls of a hurried, busy, stress-filled life. Nobody displays photos of money. And nobody decorates his home with pictures of another day at the office. Instead, on our walls, we celebrate family, friends, and faith in a better world.

But then, for some reason, we head out the door to live hurried lives of desperation. We rush from one appointment to another, hoping to find a better life through worldly gain. And each day, we pile anxiety upon anxiety.

Meanwhile, the pictures on our walls invite us to something better. They remind us of a life lived on purpose, with meaning. And they call for us to focus on the very things that make us human. Or at least they should.

Let's be intentional about what we choose to communicate with the decorations on our walls and the culture we set in our home—starting first in the space where we spend so much time together.

People First

If the relationships matter in our lives (and of course they do—very much),
then there's something special, almost sacred, about the primary gathering
spaces in our homes: the living and family rooms. Are they inviting? Are they
peaceful? Are they comfortable? Do they facilitate connections among people?
Do they help us become the kind of people we want to be? If not, then minimizing can almost miraculously bring them back to the purposes for which
they exist.

You don't need more space. You need less stuff.
#minimalisthome

I've said that getting rid of unnecessary objects enables the objects you do
keep to gain in significance; their beauty, usefulness, and originality are more
easily appreciated. But I would even go so far as to say that the *people* in a minimized home stand out more as valuable than they do in a cluttered, overcrowded house. Somehow we can *see* each other better when not distracted by
things. We are drawn to one another and are there for one another.

The names of the living room and family room are revealing. *Life* is supposed to take place there. The *family* is supposed to be formed there. So minimize the public-private spaces in your home, and watch how love wells up
within them.

Minimizing Checklist

How will you know when you've cleared out enough clutter and excess from
your living room and family room or great room? Ask yourself these questions:

- ☐ Is this space calming? Does it reduce stress?
- ☐ Does this space encourage conversation?

☐ Is this space inviting to my family? To my friends?

☐ Is this space easy to maintain?

☐ Does this space highlight what is important to our family?

☐ Does this space encourage my family to live life to the fullest?

☐ Does this space promote our family's values?

4

Personal Refuge

Decluttering the Bedrooms and Guest Room

Rachel Payne lives in Washington State with her husband and three daughters. A few years ago, Rachel's husband, Rico, an air force reservist, was deployed for a five-month assignment at Travis Air Force Base in California. During this time, he was assigned to accommodations modeled after an extended-stay hotel room. A room with a bed, a love seat, a couch, a desk, and a small kitchenette would be home for the duration of the assignment.

Back at home with the kids, Rachel expected to hear tones of frustration from Rico whenever he called her and talked about his new living arrangements. After all, he had left all the comforts of his large house with its expansive furnishings. But what she actually heard surprised her.

During their evening phone calls, Rico would comment on how much he was getting done; how unbelievably focused he felt; how little time he spent cleaning up, even turning down the cleaning service; and how little he missed "all the stuff piled up at home." Over the course of the months away, he even began to talk about making changes at home—throwing everything away and starting all over in their approach to material possessions.

Rachel couldn't wait to visit him when the opportunity arose to experience firsthand this new living space he couldn't get enough of. Her opportunity came later that year when she was able to visit him for a week.

At the base housing, Rachel saw for herself the carefree living that Rico had described to her. "Over the course of that week," she told me later, "we didn't plan a lot of vacation-style outings. We just wanted to spend time together, and that is exactly what we did. We spent a lot of time in his room, and I enjoyed the calming nature of the environment. I read a lot. And we talked a lot."

Her words resonated deeply within me as I asked for more details about her experience and emotions. She summed it up this way: "I got a little taste of what life could be like with fewer possessions in my house. I couldn't wait to get home. I wanted my home and my living space to become a sanctuary for rest and focus."

And that is exactly what she did when she returned. Starting with cloth-

---

Inspiration

A CALMER, HEALTHIER ME

One of my colleagues tells me she thinks I am the most ethical person she knows because I am always trying to save the environment. Despite trying to be as environmentally responsible as possible, I still accumulated far more than I needed, particularly in the bedroom. That was, until two years ago, when I minimized the possessions in my bedroom. Today it is much calmer, a sanctuary.

I started by removing clothes and shoes from my closet. But my efforts didn't end there. I removed makeup, books, magazines, knick-knacks, jewelry, even storage tools like shelving and boxes. Eventually I removed dressers and chairs, stand-up mirrors, and bookcases as well. Every time I opened up some space, I loved it and wanted more.

What's interesting is that I always used to be late getting into bed. I wasn't necessarily productive in the evening, more wasteful actually: watching TV or just puttering around the house until after midnight. But

ing and the bedroom, then moving to other parts of the home later, Rachel got rid of "a ton of stuff." She and her husband have continued thinning more and more over time. "We no longer want to be burdened by excess stuff," she said.

And to think it all started with one week spent in an uncluttered hotel room.

A hotel room may not be exactly your model for the bedrooms in your home. But you, too, can have more peaceful, restful bedrooms if you focus on removing unnecessary objects. A study led by clinical psychologist Pamela Thacher discovered that hoarders have worse sleep than others, and even among those who aren't hoarders, the greater their clutter, the more likely they are to have a sleep disorder.[1] This confirms what I've long believed: quality sleep in an

---

the more minimized my bedroom became, the more I desired to be in it because it was so calming to me after hard days at work. I began spending more time in the evening reading books in my room, which resulted in falling asleep faster and sleeping more soundly.

But the story doesn't end there. Because I was falling asleep more quickly, I had more energy. Soon I wanted to feel fitter. I started going to the gym and began a strength-training program. I also started eating healthier and dealing with my stress in more positive ways (yoga or walks in the park).

To top it off, in 2016, I ran a Tough Mudder race for the charity Alzheimer Scotland. This is something I would never even have contemplated before, much less been able to complete. I am learning new things about myself all the time. Minimalism for me is an ongoing journey because life is.

—Nicola, Scotland

uncluttered environment recharges all of us to go out and face another day with courage and energy.

Our home is a refuge from the world. Our bedroom is a refuge-within-the-refuge. Let's make it better through minimizing.

Remembering the Why of Your Bedrooms

The average number of bedrooms in a US home currently stands at about 3.3, a number that has been creeping up over the years.[2] This increase has come in spite of the fact that the number of family households with children under the age of eighteen living at home has been dropping significantly over the past few decades—from around 56 percent of all family households in 1970 to about 43 percent in 2015.[3]

How many bedrooms do you have in your home? Think of the space they take up. Minimize them all, and you'll have a big percentage of your house already done!

To begin, think about your purposes for the bedrooms in your home—just as we did for the living and family rooms. The master bedroom is probably mostly for rest and intimacy with your spouse, though you may also use it for such things as reading or study. If you have kids, they, too, need calming rooms to go back to for downtime, for play, to do homework, and to sleep at night. Similarly, if you have a guest room, this is a place you can offer your overnight guests to relax in private and get a good night's sleep while they're away from home.

As you focus your attention on minimizing your bedrooms, look at the possessions and ask yourself often, *Do we need this item? Does it help the room accomplish one of its purposes by providing service, beauty, or meaning?*

Remembering the purpose of your bedroom won't automatically remove the clutter, but it will provide a framework for your decision-making process. For example, in the master bedroom, does the television on your dresser promote rest or intimacy, or does it detract from these goals? (We'll be getting to that one in greater depth soon.) Is the pile of magazines or books in the corner helpful to you? Does that cluttered nightstand or top of your dresser bring you calm and relaxation?

Use the same evaluation process for the kids' bedrooms (if any) in the home. In your young son's bedroom, are there so many toys scattered about that he can't find the toy he really wants to play with—and might even trip over the debris on the floor and hurt himself? Is your daughter getting in the bad habit of turning on the TV in her room while she's studying? Does an unfinished project in your teen's room give him a sense of burden about what he still needs to do?

And then there's your guest room. Have you placed a piece of furniture in this room not because an overnight guest will need it but because you couldn't think of any other place to put it? Are you using the guest room closet as overflow storage for things you can't fit somewhere else but "might need" someday? And if so, does that excess storage keep your guests from feeling welcomed and valued?

★ STEP-BY-STEP MINIMIZING FOR YOUR BEDROOMS

I'll be getting to clothes closets in the next chapter because they present some special challenges of their own. Right now, we're learning how to minimize everything in a bedroom except the clothes closet.

As you attack your bedroom's clutter, be thoughtful, be methodical, and be confident you'll get it done.

1. Relocate Things That Don't Belong Where They Are

Are there items in a bedroom that you should keep elsewhere? For example, maybe a pile of paperwork belongs in your home office instead of your master bedroom. Or some books belong on a shelf in the family room instead of on a nightstand. Or some toys belong in the basement instead of your child's bedroom floor. Put them where they belong before focusing on what's left in the bedroom.

2. Clear the Floors

Leave nothing on the floors except for furniture (and I'm going to challenge you on that in a minute). Think beyond picking up dirty clothes. Consider also storage containers, book piles, exercise equipment, or items placed in your bedrooms temporarily that have begun to make themselves at home long term. Which of these things can you throw out, donate, or sell?

As you declutter other spaces in your bedrooms, such as drawers, you will find more space to store some of the things that are littering your floors. You may need to stack some items out of your way temporarily, until the space becomes available for them.

3. Clear Surfaces

Minimize items on your dressers, nightstands, and any shelving in the bedrooms. These might include souvenirs, decorations, crafts, plants, piles of paper, and photos. You don't need to eliminate everything from these surfaces, of course, but too often a flat surface becomes a magnet for clutter, so don't hold back in your removal process.

Keep out your most treasured items—those items that help you relax or recall happy memories. Remove anything from your sight that distracts you or stirs up anxiety, regret, or guilt.

4. Decide How to Use Closets and Drawers

I know some people who store all their clothes in the closet and have eliminated the need for a dresser. And I know others, without closet space, who choose to store clothes in dresser drawers. But one thing I have found to be consistently true—the fewer clothes you keep, the more options you have for storing them in an uncluttered manner.

If you plan to use drawers, define each of their purposes. In my house, I keep one drawer for underwear and socks, one drawer for workout clothes, and one drawer for warmer wear (mainly sweaters). Everything else I store in my closet. My wife has a similar strategy.

5. Simplify Your Bed Linens

Somewhere in your home, perhaps in a linen closet, you keep your store of sheets and blankets. Pull them all out and sort through them. Throw out all that are in poor condition or that you no longer need.

This is an ideal opportunity for using the minimalism accelerator of eliminating duplicates. Do you really need more than two sets of sheets per bed, one in use and one either in storage or in the laundry? We own just one set of bedding for each bed in our home—we just wash and return the same day. A few extra blankets may be useful on those chilly nights, but if you've accumulated more than your household would ever use at one time, the extras can go.

6. Pare Down Your Decorations

I wrote in the last chapter about the importance of choosing wisely the decorations we keep in our home and on our walls. Extend the same philosophy to your bedroom environments. Reject decorations that simply match the colors of a bedspread; choose instead to portray images with meaning that direct your attention toward things that matter. You will free up both physical space and mental focus.

7. Get Rid of Furniture, If Possible

Prior to being introduced to minimalism, Kim and I had five pieces of furniture in our room: a bed, a dresser, two nightstands, and one large armoire upon which our television sat. The armoire was filled with my clothing, while my wife stored hers in the dresser. We also shared the closet—her clothes on the left side, mine on the right side. As we began decluttering our bedroom, we removed many of the clothing items from our closet, dresser, and armoire. We also removed our television. Because of those changes, without any inconvenience whatsoever, we were able to remove the large armoire from our room, instantly creating a great deal of new openness in the room.

Maybe you have a piece of furniture—or more than one—you can remove from your bedroom or one of the other bedrooms in the house. Nothing else will make as big an impact in minimizing a bedroom as getting rid of furniture.

8. Make the Best Use of Under-the-Bed Space

The problem with most under-the-bed spaces is that they quickly become places for hoarding more and more unnecessary things. Our closets are full, our drawers are full . . . and the next available space is under the bed. So that space quickly collects countless items, seemingly never to be seen again by human eyes.

Let's be clear—that's *not* what I am talking about when I encourage you to use the under-the-bed space. I am talking about being intentional with the items you keep there.

I use the space under my bed for storing useful items that I do not want to leave out in the open. Under my side of the bed, I store the books I am currently reading. This keeps them within arm's reach but does not leave clutter on a nightstand. (Actually, there is no nightstand there. I removed the one from my side of the bed—the second piece of master bedroom furniture we discarded.) I also keep some business files under my bed. My wife keeps a few boxes of keepsakes under her side as well. We live in a house with no basement or attic, so using that space under the bed has been helpful to us.

Rethinking the Bedroom TV

As I mentioned, my wife and I got rid of our bedroom television. It was the single biggest step we took toward improving rest and intimacy in our bedroom. And because of our experience, I hope that you'll strongly consider making the same decision.

What we think about first in our day and what we think about last really matters. Every morning begins with a clean slate and brand-new opportunities. We would be wise to think carefully about whether we want television

Minimalist Home Value

REST

Consider the benefits that rest offers: a healthier body, less stress, deeper relationships, opportunity to evaluate life's direction, a fresh outlook on life, creation of better life balance, and even increased productivity.

Any physician will tell you rest is essential for physical health. When the body is deprived of sleep, it is unable to rebuild and recharge itself adequately. Your *body* requires rest.

Any athlete will tell you rest is essential for physical training. Rest is needed for muscles to repair themselves and prevent injury. This is true whether you run marathons, pitch baseballs, or climb rocks. Your *muscles* require rest.

Yesterday's great thinkers will tell you rest is essential for clear thinking. Ovid, the Roman poet, said, "Take rest; a field that has rested gives a bountiful crop."[4] Your *mind* requires rest.

Most religious leaders will tell you rest is essential for spiritual well-being. Buddhism, Judaism, Christianity, Islam, and Baha'i (among others) teach the importance of setting aside a period of time for rest. Your *soul* requires rest.

Many corporate leaders will tell you, similarly, that rest is essential on the job. Rest increases productivity, replenishes attention, solidifies memories, and encourages creativity.[5] Your pursuit of *work* requires rest.

The wise and knowledgeable tell us the same thing: take time to rest.

A minimalist home is one that promotes peace, serenity, relaxation, calmness, and sleep—rest, in other words. And no place in the home is more necessary to rest than the bedroom.

producers to decide what thoughts to fill our minds with as we start our day. The evening provides valuable opportunity to meditate and assess our day. Unfortunately, many people sacrifice this opportunity for the sake of televised entertainment.

Not having a television in the bedroom also encourages getting more and better sleep. We know that Americans, on average, watch an incredible 35.5 hours of television per week, and this shows us how hard it is for us to turn off the TV at any point in the day, including bedtime.[6] Not only does television in the bedroom keep us up later at night, but watching television before bed also disrupts our sleep cycles.[7]

With no television in the bedroom, you and your spouse will have more conversations—some of the most important conversations of your day. In his book *Two in a Bed,* social scientist Paul Rosenblatt said, "Bedtime is not just about sleep. It is about renewing and maintaining the couple relationship. It can be the one time when partners learn what has been going on with one another, plan, make decisions, deal with disagreements, solve problems, provide necessary information, and put words to their realities."[8] That kind of bedtime contact is compromised when the television is on.

According to some studies, couples who keep a TV in the bedroom have sex half as often as those who don't.[9] Why? Probably because there are over a million things more stimulating for a woman than a man watching ESPN's *SportsCenter.*

If you ask me, the opportunity for more intimate encounters should be reason enough to get rid of a bedroom TV. But if it isn't, here are even more benefits we discovered to eliminating the television from the bedroom:

- less electricity usage
- less space taken up in our room
- more time for reading
- less distraction when getting ready in the morning
- a better example for our kids

Still not quite convinced you should get rid of the TV in your bedroom? Commit to trying it out as a twenty-nine-day experiment. Unplugging the television and moving it into a different room will take fewer than five minutes. There is an end in sight. You've got nothing to lose and maybe a whole lot to gain.

Perspectives for Minimizing Kids' Bedrooms

Kids' bedrooms can be some of the trickier places to minimize in the home. Not more tricky physically. More tricky relationally.

Kids can benefit as much, if not more, from minimalism as grown-ups can because they have longer to reap the rewards of good habits after they depart from their childhood home. Can you imagine going back and living life over *not buying* all the stuff you're getting rid of today? You may not be able to go back and start again, but your kids can start out right!

At the same time, however, as parents we don't want to force behaviors on our kids in such a way that they come to resent it, possibly contributing to a reaction that's worse than bedroom messiness. We want our kids to feel at home in their rooms, but at the same time we hope they will choose to incorporate simplicity into their daily living patterns and their self-expression within their rooms.

It's tricky, but it's not impossible to navigate successfully among the risks when it comes to minimizing kids' bedrooms.

Minimize Your Own Bedroom First

With kids, minimalism is better caught than taught. As parents, we need to be modeling the removal of unneeded possessions and a refusal to buy new stuff that will just waste money and clutter up the home. This means, among other things, that you should declutter the master bedroom first, allowing your kids to see that you're willing to eliminate a bunch of your own personal stuff.

When you've done that, you will have more credibility with them when you talk about minimizing their bedrooms.

Remember a Kid's Bedroom Is Like His or Her "Home"

Kids don't just sleep in their bedrooms. They keep toys and games there and invite friends into their rooms to play. They experiment with their "look," trying out different clothes and makeup. They do craft projects or pursue hobbies. They read and study. They may keep a computer there. They like to bring in pets. In a way, they reproduce many of the adult functions of the home in their rooms.

So anticipate a diversity of minimizing decisions. Affirm their developing interests and tastes as well as the comfort they take in having their own private spaces. Just make sure you show them how keeping less stuff in their rooms will make their rooms better "homes" for them, where they can have even more space to discover who they are.

Use Physical Boundaries to Set Limits Without Squelching Independence

Boundaries is my term for any limit, physical or numerical, that is placed on the ownership of some category of objects. Boundaries give kids concrete limits while letting them decide how to fill up the allotted space. For example, we tell our daughter, Alexa, that she can keep whatever art supplies she wants—as long as they fit within a storage box we've given her for her room. She gets full control over which items remain and which items go. Other possible boundaries for kids' bedrooms include one cardboard box for toys, one shelf of stuffed animals, or one craft project left out at any given time.

Recognize the Bedroom TV As What It Is: A Threat to Your Child's Well-Being

As important as getting rid of the TV from the master bedroom is, it's at least as important to do the same in the kids' bedrooms.

The average youth spends roughly 900 hours in school each year—and about 1,200 hours a year watching TV! Television viewing is connected to getting less sleep, having worse academic performance, and having higher rates of obesity.[10] So if your child is among the 70 percent of kids ages eight to eighteen who have a TV set in their room or who watch television via a tablet or computer in the bedroom, you should at least set a boundary regarding its use. It's probably even better to get rid of that bedroom television altogether.

Sweet Dreams

I hope you'll dive into minimizing the bedrooms in your house, one by one, with great enthusiasm, because the benefits are huge and the task is achievable. You've already got the principles and steps you need to know to do the job. Before I leave this space, though, I want to return to the most basic purpose of all bedrooms: sleep.

We're not getting enough of it.

HOW MUCH SLEEP SHOULD YOU BE GETTING?

The following are recommended amounts of sleep for different age groups, according to the National Sleep Foundation.[11]

Newborns (0–3 months): 14–17 hours per day

Infants (4–11 months): 12–15 hours per day

Toddlers (1–2 years): 11–14 hours per day

Preschoolers (3–5 years): 10–13 hours per day

School-age children (6–13 years): 9–11 hours per day

Teenagers (14–17 years): 8–10 hours per day

Younger adults (18–25 years): 7–9 hours per day

Adults (26–64 years): 7–9 hours per day

Older adults (65+ years): 7–8 hours per day

Forty percent of people in the United States get less than the recommended amount of sleep, compared to only 11 percent of people who were sleep deprived in the 1940s.[12] According to surveys, nearly 30 percent of adults report an average of fewer than six hours of sleep per day. And only 31 percent of high school students report getting at least eight hours of sleep on an average school night.[13] Among children, research links sleep loss with fatigue, bad moods, attention problems, impaired memory, academic problems, and obesity.[14]

The sleep problem today is similar in many countries. The country where people are getting the least shut-eye? Japan.[15]

One underappreciated benefit of minimalism is the ability to walk confidently through your bedroom with the lights off. #minimalisthome

---

Our world is not good at promoting the virtue of rest. In fact, we foolishly believe we are improving our well-being by skipping out on sleep and rest for the sake of a hurried life.

Nor is rest easy to take. Although modern society loves shortcuts—fifteen-minute abs, thirty-minute meals, and one-hour photos—there are no shortcuts or microwave solutions to quality rest. It must be entered deliberately and allowed to complete its cycle in due time. This requires patience and a cleared schedule.

A decluttered bedroom is less distracting and more calming, promoting more and better sleep. And a person who wakes up rested is in a better mood and has more energy and concentration to devote to making the most of the day.

Minimizing Checklist

How will you know when you've cleared out enough clutter and excess from your bedrooms? Ask yourself these questions:

For the master bedroom . . .

☐ Does this space foster intimacy with my spouse?

☐ Do I get enough rest here?

☐ Is this a room I enjoy retreating to at night and waking up to in the morning?

For the kids' bedrooms . . .

☐ Are the kids comfortable hanging out in their rooms during the day?

☐ Are they getting enough sleep at night?

For the guest room . . .

☐ Is there enough space in my guest room to comfortably accommodate all the belongings my overnight guests bring with them?

☐ Is the space relaxing and restful for them?

Iconic

Decluttering the Clothes Closets and Mudroom

With just one word, Alice Gregory, a writer living in New York City, forever changed my view of clothing and how much of it to keep around. Writing for J. Crew a few years ago, Alice shared her decision to simplify her wardrobe to one specific style that she would wear every day—a black long-sleeve shirt and fashionable jeans. She called it her "uniform." But *uniform* isn't the word that got me.

Amid her reasons for dressing like this, she stated that having a simple outfit you are known for wearing is "iconic, it's a cheap and easy way to feel famous." *Iconic.* That's it. Minimalist clothing can convey a classic and memorable sense of personal identity.

Alice argues that wearing a similar outfit every day is a way of asserting your status as a protagonist in life. "This is the reason why characters in picture books never change their clothes: Children—like adults, if they'd only admit it—crave continuity." So along with the ease of no longer having to create a new look every day, you have the comfort of feeling like yourself all the time.

Another reason for wearing a simplified, iconic wardrobe is that it enables you to step out of the constantly swirling waters of fashion. *Is this outdated? Should I get one of those? Do I look good in this?* You can forget these worries because, as Gregory said, "Nobody thinks of a person who wears the same thing every day as unstylish. Rather, it's simply a classification that does not apply."[1]

We, of course, live in a world that promotes the opposite approach to clothing. The mantra of the present age is "More is better. Newer fashions are superior. And if you are not keeping up with the latest styles and colors, everybody is going to notice." This is the messaging we see reflected in ads, in store windows, and on television almost every day.

The prevalent attitude to fashion is downright silly, if you think about it. As Henry David Thoreau said long ago, "Every generation laughs at the old fashions, but follows religiously the new."[2] In most cases, it is classic fashion, not the trending pieces and colors, that stands the test of time.

In his later years, Albert Einstein usually wore the same suit. Steve Jobs favored a black turtleneck, jeans, and sneakers. Mark Zuckerberg likes to wear a gray T-shirt. Their reputations certainly didn't take a hit because they simplified their wardrobe decisions.

Well, those are all men. Could it be different for women?

Evidently not. Alice Gregory is doing fine with her iconic wardrobe. Similarly, Matilda Kahl, an art director for a leading New York ad agency, wears the same style of clothing to work every day and says it simplifies her morning routine while leveling the playing field with her male colleagues.[3]

My good friend Courtney Carver minimized her wardrobe down to a capsule set with only thirty-three items. She wore those same pieces over the course of several months and told me recently, "Not a single person noticed. Despite the fact that I worked at a high-end fashion magazine *and* my story was covered extensively by the Associated Press, not a single person ever raised even a question."

I'm not asking you to wear the same thing every day. Nor am I asking you to get rid of that pair of jeans that fits so perfectly or the dress you love to wear when you go out dancing. But I am suggesting that you can radically thin out the clothes in your home's closets—your own, your kids', and the mudroom or coat closet by the door—and that it will not only make your house more attractive and efficient but also make you feel more at ease.

A Better Closet

If you have a tendency to overbuy clothing, the evidence is before you every time you go to your closet, with clothes on hangers shoved so closely together that they are hard to separate, rows or piles of shoes on the floor, and sweatshirts and sweaters threatening to spill off the overhead shelves. Or check out your kids' closets—how many clothes do they have in there, and how many other items, such as toys and games?

Then there's the place where you keep coats. Is yours a place you would feel comfortable using to hang up a guest's coat while she looks on? Or is it embarrassingly overstuffed with the family's own coats, boots, hats, gloves, and scarves?

Now, I know that in those home makeover shows we see on TV one of the biggest complaints about an existing home is that the closets are too small. There's a reason why older homes have smaller clothes closets than new ones— people used to get by just fine with fewer clothes. So is the answer to buy a newer house with large closets? Or is it to reduce the number of clothes so that our wardrobes will fit in the closet space we already have? If you've been thinking you need bigger closets, maybe all you need to do is right-size your wardrobe—and your closets will feel bigger overnight.

In new homes today, closet space, on average, accounts for 146 square feet.[4] Although people used to be satisfied with reach-in closets, now there's a demand for walk-in closets, with a majority of home buyers willing to pay extra to get them.[5] Quite literally, some of us have closets as large as the size of many homes in poor countries. And in order to find the clothes they want out of the vast abundance of their wardrobe in their oversized closets, some people resort to installing closet organizing systems that cost hundreds or even thousands of dollars.

I'm not trying to lay guilt on you if you have large closets. I'm trying to help us all think that maybe we don't need more clothes or more closet space. Maybe the closet space in our current home—whatever it happens to be—is enough, if we will just reduce the quantity of our clothing to a more reasonable level. And if we choose to downsize to a smaller home at some future time, then the smaller closet space it comes with will be just right.

Consider how different your life will look when you own fewer clothes:

- You will have more time to live your life. Fewer clothes means less time getting ready. It also means less time shuffling through piles of sweaters, moving hangers full of clothes, or trying on different pairs of shoes to find the coordinating pair.

- Mornings will feature less stress. Not only will getting ready become easier and require less time, but you will also eliminate the often-overlooked anxiety of peering into a full closet and wondering what clothes you should pick out—or staring at all the clothes you feel guilty for purchasing but never wearing or wish you could fit into but haven't been the right size for in a long time.

- Packing for business trips and vacations will take less time.

- The clothes themselves will keep in better shape. An uncluttered closet is less likely to cause shoes to be stepped on, let dust accumulate on clothing, and create wrinkles.

- As you maintain a minimized wardrobe over time, buying fewer clothes will result in your having more disposable income. Even if you choose to purchase higher quality clothing in the future, you could still end up ahead in the pocketbook.

Go a different route with your clothing. Try owning fewer pieces. Contrary to what you've heard, you just don't need to buy and own a lot of clothes.

ORDER BEHIND THE WARDROBE DOORS

My wardrobes used to be chaos. Things were everywhere. I'd place clothes wherever I could fit them—often just on my dresser or piled up rather than hung up. I could never find what I was looking for. And if I did, it almost always had to be re-ironed because the clothes were shoved in so tight.

I used to have this idea that if I just shut the wardrobe doors I could pretend it was all okay. But every time I opened my wardrobe, I was reminded that it wasn't. The physical space reflected my mental chaos, or maybe it was contributing to it. Either way, I knew I needed a change.

I minimized my closet last year. I grabbed some black bags and started in one corner of my closet. I sorted my clothes into *yes*, *no*, and *maybe* piles. *Yes* items stayed. *No* items went. And when I finished, I also decided that my entire *maybe* pile would be donated to charity. I found I built momentum as I began to get rid of things and kept going. The more I got rid of, the more decisive I became.

It's unbelievable how the process has affected my mood each morning and evening. I spend much less time cleaning, and my dresser is clear. It means I can actually sit down at my dresser and get ready peacefully. I now have a clear chair too so I can lay out my clothes for the next day the night before, which makes morning decisions easier.

Less time stressing about clothes and ironing has left me extra time in the morning, which I can now spend on reading, meditation, or a slower breakfast. It's nice having space—both physically and mentally—to center my day before it even begins.

—Selina, England

Who Says We Need Changing
Fashion, Anyway?

A few months after I started my minimalism journey, a headline on my computer caught my attention: "Top 10 Colors Define a Season of Change." According to the article, "the Fall '08 palette is best described as a season of change and is defined by rich, elegant hues that offer a vibrant selection. New York's fashion designers emphasize cooler blues, greens and purples in the top five tones used in their collections, followed by variations of warm red, orange and yellow."[6]

I wondered, *Who gets to decide what the must-have colors are going to be for fall 2008?* I mean, is there a committee somewhere that makes these kinds of decisions? Does it just so happen that a large number of people are enthusiastically drawn to the same colors at the same time? Or is there something else happening here? Is this an orchestrated effort?

It occurred to me that, if I were running the fashion industry, it would be helpful for me to change the in-fashion colors and styles often. This way, people would have to buy new clothes to keep up with the trends, which would result in more money flowing into my industry. All parts of the supply chain would benefit: designers, manufacturers, retailers, and anyone else who makes a living off the selling of clothes.

This is just what's happening. If the fashion industry wasn't intentionally telling us that our old clothes were out of style, we'd probably stop buying their product. After all, we already have enough clothes in our closet to last quite some time.

The US apparel industry today is a $12 billion business, and the average American family spends $1,700 on clothes annually.[7] On average, that's 3.5 percent of a family's expenses—arguably not much—but what's more significant is whether that money is spent on need or waste. The answer, largely, is waste. Americans throw away 13 million tons of textiles each year, accounting for 9 percent of total nonrecycled waste.[8]

It hasn't always been like that. Our appetite for clothing is demonstrably growing. According to *Forbes,* "In 1930, the average American woman owned nine outfits. In 2015 that figure was 30 outfits—one for every day of the month."[9] The same trend is occurring in Britain, where in 2006 "women bought twice as many clothes as they had just ten years earlier."[10] *The Daily Mail* reports that the average woman in the United Kingdom has twenty-two items in her closet that she will never wear but refuses to throw out.[11]

Among its other drawbacks, the practice of overbuying clothes is expensive. About half of US women have between $1,000 and $5,000 worth of clothing and shoes in their closets. The fashion magazine that reported these numbers also said, "A lucky 9 percent report having apparel and accessories that total over $10,000."[12] Lucky? Well, that's one way to look at it. These same women also have over $10,000 less in their savings accounts.

If you need nice things to impress your friends, you have the wrong friends. #minimalisthome

---

Incredibly to me, one study revealed "women have fashion on the brain 91 times in a given day—that's more than four times the amount that men think about sex.[13]

I don't mean to pick on women. Men make too much of fashion and hang on to too many clothes as well. (I should know, because when I became a minimalist, I got rid of an embarrassing number of my own items of clothing.) Ties dating back to the previous decade, if not century. Dress clothes that we might wear if we have the right sort of business meeting. Shoes for more occasions than we'll ever actually encounter. Men can be clothes hoarders just as much as women.

So I have to ask, is all this clothes buying and storing benefiting our lives in any way?

In his well-known book *The Paradox of Choice,* Barry Schwartz argued that it is not. He said, "Freedom and autonomy are critical to our well-being, and choice is critical to freedom and autonomy. Nonetheless, though modern Americans have more choice than any group of people ever has had before, and thus, presumably, more freedom and autonomy, we don't seem to be benefiting from it psychologically."[14] His argument, stated throughout the book and re-produced in studies, is that more choice does not mean better living.

As choice increases, so does paralysis of decision. Ever stare into a full closet of clothes and still have no idea what to wear? As options increase, so does the sense of bewilderment and frustration. Additionally, an abundance of choice often results in less satisfaction and sometimes poorer decisions.

It would seem from everything we've been told that more clothes hanging in our closets would lead to a happier life. But psychologically and scientifically, that is simply not the case. In fact, often, more choice leads to less happiness— the paradox of choice. Not to mention the unending frustration of having to keep up with ever-changing trends.

Maybe getting our money makes the leaders of the fashion industry happy. But buying excessive quantities of their products isn't doing the same for us.

Running with the Cool Kids

Sometimes the reason we buy more clothes than we need doesn't have to do with external forces or advertisements. Sometimes the reason is internal.

In high school, I played tennis and my favorite class was accounting. I found out pretty early that the tennis team didn't get invited to many parties. Neither did the accountants, unfortunately.

On the other hand, my twin brother was a star on the football team, the basketball team, and the track team, and his social life reflected his status. He was a popular figure at those parties I never got into.

I had plenty of free time, while sitting alone at home, to long for the day when being one of the cool kids didn't matter. Some days I think I'm still wait-ing. And apparently I'm not the only one.

Once I was in a clothing store with my wife because I needed new pants. I was not the only one using the dressing rooms. In fact, I wasn't even the only one asking my wife for her opinion. As I emerged from one of the dressing rooms wearing a khaki pair of pants, I noticed a young female shopper striking up a conversation with my wife.

The shopper began, "Do you think this shirt looks good on me? I think it looks a little boxy."

"Yeah, you're right. It does look a little boxy on you," my wife answered.

The young woman went on, "Yeah, I know. It's just that everybody is wearing this style now. Honestly, I just like wearing T-shirts and jeans. I really don't know what to do."

In my mind, the answer was simple: It doesn't matter what everyone else is wearing. Buy the type of clothing you like best. Spend your money on something you really love and need, not the current fashion trends in the magazines—especially if you don't feel like yourself in them.

But I know it's not always that easy.

The pull toward conformity can be strong. The desire to fit in with popular culture is significant at times, as is the desire to impress others with our clothing. And no matter how old we get, the desire to run with the cool kids can remain.

But I believe that within each of us is a desire that is even stronger—the desire to be ourselves, to embrace the things we love and enjoy and that make us unique. One of the best decisions we can make is to reject the cultural expectations that change with the wind. And to accept the fact that we don't need to run with the cool kids to be happy.

We can choose to be ourselves instead. Our clothes can be a reflection of that.

★ STEP-BY-STEP MINIMIZING FOR YOUR CLOTHES CLOSETS

Whether you are hoping to reduce your clothing to a "uniform" or just trying to pare down your wardrobe to gain more efficiency, now's the time to give your crowded closet a break. Get ready to ask about the contents of your closets, *Do I really need this?*

1. Consider Removing Non-Clothes Items

Sometimes, whether for convenience or by accident, non-clothes items collect in our clothes closets. Toys littering the floor of a kid's closet. Hockey sticks leaned against the inside wall of a coat closet. A wedding album resting on a shelf in the master bedroom closet.

Having things other than clothes in your closets is fine, if that's what you want. But take a look at what you've got in the closets, and see if some items

---

CREATING AN ANTI-DIDEROT EFFECT

Named for an eighteenth-century French philosopher, the *Diderot effect* describes the tendency for one purchase to lead to others. We see this effect in operation in many places around the home. First a dog, then a bunch of dog supplies. First a fishing pole, then tackle boxes full of fishing gear.

Perhaps the place in our homes where we most clearly see the Diderot effect operating is in our wardrobes as clothing purchases lead to other clothing or accessory purchases. "I'm going to have to get shoes to match this suit." "I really need a new necklace to go with this new top." It's almost a reflex—one purchase leads to another.

Minimalism enables us to reverse this trend. If you reduce the number of your clothes and are keeping fewer colors and styles, this automatically reduces the number of accessories that match your look. It works the other way too—reduce the number of your accessories, and that will help you decide to get rid of the clothes that require the accessories you've removed.

might belong better in other parts of the house, such as toys in the toy room or sports gear on the garage shelves.

As before, relocate such items. Now you're ready to tackle the main thing: your clothes.

2. Set a Goal for Your Clothing Reduction

Do you want to remove a quarter of your clothing? Maybe a third?

According to the National Association of Productivity and Organizing Professionals most people wear 20 percent of the clothes they own 80 percent of the time (the Pareto Principle in action).[15] You don't need to get rid of 80 percent of your clothing the first time through your closet, but knowing this statistic, surely you could get rid of a lot, couldn't you?

3. Categorize Your Clothing and Start Giving Things Away

Three types of clothing usually make up our wardrobes:

- the clothes we love to wear
- the clothes we never wear
- the clothes we kind of like and wear occasionally

Notice the style and color of the clothes you naturally tend to reach for in the closet. These must be the clothes you feel more comfortable and confident in, right? So begin to create your iconic fashion style around those pieces.

On the other hand, if an item of clothing in your closet doesn't fit you anymore, you don't like it, or you don't remember the last time you wore it, don't hesitate—get rid of it. I'm not saying that you couldn't see yourself conceivably wearing it at some point, but if you haven't *actually* been wearing it, then it's unlikely you would wear it much in the future either, and there's little point in keeping it around.

This brings us to the questionable pieces in your closet, those that you rarely wear but aren't sure you're ready to part with. Let me say this: probably it would be better if you got rid of the majority of these clothes. But I know it can be hard to decide, and so to help you figure out which ones to keep and which ones to remove, try this fun experiment:

Turn around all the hangers in your closet so the open side of the handle is facing toward you. When you return a piece of clothing that you've worn to a hanger, place it back on the rod with the handle curving away from you, so you know at a glance you've worn this piece. After a set period of time, remove every article of clothing on a hanger that is still pointing toward you. You may want to consider one or two months as a good time for your current season's clothes. And then start the experiment again once a new season begins. These are the clothes you haven't worn since you started the experiment. I guess you don't really need them, do you?

By the way, I would strongly discourage you from removing clothes belonging to your spouse without permission. Clothes preferences are highly personal. Minimize your own side of the closet, and leave it up to your spouse to decide what to get rid of from his or her own wardrobe.

The same advice holds for older children. Encourage teens to minimize their closets, but let them make the choices themselves. Praise them when they choose to let go of unneeded pieces.

With younger children, you can be more directive. Create a clothing boundary. For example, say, "You can have as many hanging clothes as will conveniently fit on this one rod—you choose what they are," or, "Let's pick ten things from your closet that you want to donate today."

4. Keep Only One Size—the Size That Fits You Now

If you've gained weight, should you keep your older, smaller clothes as motivation to reduce weight?

Courtney Carver said, "Multiple sizes may feel like a safety net, but they may also be a painful reminder of how you feel in your own skin. There's no proof that smaller sizes encourage you to lose weight and the stress of trying could even contribute to weight gain. Keep one size in your closet and take a walk with the extra time you save in the morning when deciding what to wear."[16]

5. Reduce Your Accessories

It's not just hanging clothes you need to thin out from your closets. There are also the hats, shoes, belts, purses, ties, scarves, gloves, jewelry, and other items you use to accessorize your look. We tend to accumulate a lot of these, especially as they are frequent gifts. Eventually our set of accessories can go from being a treasured but limited collection to rivaling a department store display table full of items we never wear.

Apply the same *love to use, never use,* and *occasionally use* categories to your accessories, getting rid of all the never used and as many of the occasionally used accessories as you can. If you've already reduced the number of your clothes and are keeping fewer colors and styles, this automatically reduces the number of accessories that match your look and thus will help you decide which pieces to get rid of.

In fact, you might consider going the other way and using your accessories to help you decide which items of clothing to get rid of. For example, when I minimized my closet, I decided to sharply reduce my number of accessories by keeping only one color: black. I removed all my brown belts and shoes and watches. With this new baseline accessory color, I kept only clothes that matched black accessories. The same strategy could also work for jewelry—you don't need a bunch of duplicates in all these categories.

Limit your accessories, and then you can more easily limit your clothes and have easier decisions when making new clothing purchases. (I know this is the opposite of the way many of us think about clothing and accessories—we pick the clothes first and then get accessories to match. But then minimalism is contrarian by nature.)

The Shirt Off Your Back

Stacy is a thirty-five-year-old wife and mother of two who made a decision to simplify her life and begin focusing on things that matter. After I finished a speaking engagement, she approached me to tell her story.

"I have done very well, Joshua. I have slowly worked through most of the rooms in my home, throwing out most of my husband's stuff," she said with a laugh and a smile. "No, honestly, I've done well and am proud of my progress. Except for one area of my home—I felt frozen and stuck contemplating the idea of removing clothes and shoes from the closet. I have always prided myself on being current with fashions and styles, and working through that area of my home was always going to be difficult."

That was, until the week before we met. She continued with her story: "Just last week, I was driving downtown toward work and noticed something I had never seen before. Our local battered-women's shelter was not all that far from my corporate office park, and yet I had never noticed it before. As I thought about the facility, my mind raced to the women who called it home. It occurred to me that within those walls were dozens of women, many of whom had probably left their homes in the middle of the night with nothing but the clothes on their backs and their children in their arms, seeking shelter and help and a new life."

She continued with tears welling up in her eyes. "I immediately began to think of the rows and rows of clothes and shoes sitting idly in my closet at home. I began to consider how much beauty and dignity those articles of clothing could bestow upon those women. How they could be used by the women for job interviews or providing a splash of confidence on their first day of work.

"And in that moment, Joshua, I found everything I needed to finally declutter my closet. The process wasn't just about me trying to improve my life anymore; it was about using my excess, unused clothing to become a blessing to others."

For the clothes that you will minimize, the usual categories of trash, recycle, sell, and donate apply. But especially in this case I think it's usually best to donate it, just as Stacy did. That strategy does good for others and gets the excess clothing out of your house quickly. Generosity in this case is not just the byproduct of minimalism; it is also the motivation for it.

Take any used clothing that's in good condition to one of the national-chain nonprofits or a local nonprofit that will use or resell it. Get a receipt and deduct the value from your taxes. In the United States, IRS Publication 561 gives guidelines for determining the value of donated clothing (and other goods).

For textiles that can no longer be salvaged, you may have to put them in

---

Minimalist Home Value

BEING YOURSELF

The ancient philosopher Lao Tzu is credited with saying, "Care about what other people think, and you will always be their prisoner."

Minimizing your clothing collection is not about giving up on looking your best. But it *is* about not trying to impress others through slavishly following fashion. That's like chasing the wind.

Today's fashions look better on airbrushed models than on "real people." Buying clothes is costly. Even if you get them and they look good, soon they'll seem dated. And maybe they never really express who you are.

Our clothes "speak." They say something about who we are and what we believe and how we want to be thought of. Today's latest fashions may say something that's consistent with another person's identity but not yours. Even if they seem appropriate for you, fashions are going to change in no time.

It's much better to stick to clothes that are comfortable, that give you confidence, and that look good on you, regardless of whether they're showing up on the covers of fashion magazines these days.

Wearing a simple and iconic wardrobe lets *you* be the star of your life's drama. Not your clothes.

---

the trash, but there are also a number of recycling opportunities. Some organizations recycle old textiles and break down the material into insulation products, carpet padding, paper, or yarn. Some pet shelters will use the old materials for cleaning materials or bedding. And some Goodwill stores will accept your worn-out clothing and sell it to salvage brokers or make it into industrial wipes.

Before we leave the topic of clothing and how much of it we store in our homes, let's consider one special place some homes have.

Its Name Is Mud

A mudroom is a way station between inside and outside. For rainy days, muddy days, or snowy days, in particular, it's a valuable place to have in a home to put on your coat, boots, hat, and gloves, or to take them off again. A mudroom typically has a bench for sitting on when dressing with your outerwear, and it may be equipped with cabinets, shelves, and coat hooks or hangers on a rod. It's usually positioned at the back or side door, though sometimes at the front door.

Not every house has a mudroom, but if yours has one, you know that it is basically utilitarian: it stores outerwear and keeps mud and dirt from being tracked into the house. But it can also have some warm memories associated with it. This might be where Mom helped her little ones get bundled up to go out and make their first snowman. This could be where you greet guests and take their coats when they come over for your annual Christmas Eve party.

To make your mudroom a place of charm and convenience, rather than of clutter and frustration, pull out every object in it and decide what you can do with it. Have some items settled here that don't really belong? Relocate them. How about decorations that now seem to your newly minimalistic eyes to be excessive? Eliminate them. Are there clothing items that duplicate the purpose of other items—more than one coat for each season per person, for example? Or that don't fit the wearer anymore? Or that just never get used? Is there furniture that is just taking up space? Or are there other large items getting in the way of the room's function more than contributing to it? Donate them to others who will be grateful for them.

Once you've settled on what to keep in your mudroom, the key becomes tidiness. Make sure everything you keep is where it belongs—Dad's parka on a hook, the kids' snow boots under the bench, hats on the top shelf, umbrella in the stand, or whatever you decide. Day after day, as you make your stop in this way station, you'll love how much better your mudroom works for you. And you'll notice how your kids will get better at keeping it tidy when everything has a specific home.

Our home in Vermont didn't have a mudroom, but it did have an entryway with a coat closet. After we minimized the coat closet, I noticed it got used more often. When we had to cram our coats into the closet every time we wanted to hang something, it was easy to just throw them on the floor. But when there was space in the closet, hanging coats was easier, quicker, and happened more often. Same with storing shoes on the floor of the coat closet. When countless things were piled up because the shelves were already too full of other stuff, nobody used the floor of the coat closet for shoes. But there was a noticeable change when we minimized that closet—my kids at the time were quite young and yet did a good job of putting things away inside it.

The Real You

A survey conducted by IKEA in Canada reported that about a third of customers were more satisfied after cleaning out their closets than after sex.[17] I can't promise you those kinds of results, but I think you'll be surprised by how much of a relief it is to go to your closet and find it spacious and orderly.

Your clothes closets don't have to be a source of stress. When you've minimized the closets, their contents don't need a lot of updating. Your clothing selection doesn't remind you of times when you weighed less, or false personas you once tried on, or money you blew at clothing shops. You don't have to waste time sorting through the options and asking yourself every day what you feel like wearing. A minimized closet makes for easier living.

Even more so, I know you're going to love walking out the door wearing your own iconic fashion made up of clothes that fit well, flatter you, and are as comfortable as an old friendship. Doesn't that sound lovely? To be confident about your own personal style, as opposed to worrying about whether the fashion has changed without you? The *you* whom you present to the world is the real you, comfortable in your own skin . . . and in your own clothing.

Minimizing Checklist

How will you know when you've cleared out enough clutter and excess from your clothes closets and mudroom? Ask yourself these questions:

For the master bedroom closet . . .

- ☐ Is my closet filled only with clothes I love to wear?
- ☐ Are there any clothes in my closet left over from a previous season of life that I still need to remove?
- ☐ Does my clothes closet empower me to make quick, confident decisions about what to wear in the morning?
- ☐ Have I left enough space in my closet for my clothes to hang freely?

For the other closets in the home . . .

- ☐ Does everything in this closet belong and have a designated space?
- ☐ Are the other members of my household catching on to the advantages of having a neat and streamlined closet?

For the mudroom . . .

- ☐ Is the coat closet or mudroom a tidy, efficient stopping place between indoors and outdoors?
- ☐ Is my family inclined to put things away because there is room for them now?

Clean Sweep

Decluttering the Bathrooms and Laundry Room

Now we come to spaces that have some of the humblest purposes in the home: keeping our bodies and our clothes clean. Our bathrooms and laundry room might not seem important, but since we use them so frequently, letting them stay cluttered would mean embracing aggravation and inefficiency every day. Minimizing these spaces restores their ability to fulfill their intended purposes. And at least in the case of the bathroom, eliminating clutter can give us a feeling of peace that calms our spirits.

If we are to believe some advertisements, the ideal master bathroom is a vast space with gleaming tile, shining fixtures, and spouting fountains, where beautiful people pamper themselves or luxuriate in baths amid drooping palms and flickering candles. None of us actually have a bathroom like that, but we can still dream of retreating to one that offers us a sense of privacy and repose. With that in mind, the makeover your bathroom needs is not more square footage and newer fixtures; it is a removal of all the excess stuff that's giving it that messy, distracting look. I don't know how big your master bathroom is, but get rid of the clutter, and I guarantee it will *seem* more spacious. You'll begin to enjoy greater calm and relaxation right in the bathroom you've already got.

In the old days, before we minimized our bathroom, I used to get annoyed when my hands knocked over a tube of antiperspirant sitting beside my sink, or a bottle of hair gel fell off the shelf when I reached into our bathroom cabinet. That kind of thing hardly ever happens anymore. I can calmly, yet quickly, do whatever I came to the bathroom to do. In other words, every day I appreciate the benefits of bathroom minimizing.

You, too, can enjoy the benefits of made-over bathrooms and laundry room in your home through minimizing.

It's an Experience

We love our bathrooms. In the United States, even though the average household size has been gradually shrinking for decades, the number of bathrooms in the typical home has continued to increase. In 1973, the norm was one bathroom. By 2012, the average number of bathrooms in a single-family US home had risen to 2.56 bathrooms.[1] Most Britons and Aussies also look for homes with at least two bathrooms.[2]

Referring to the number of bathrooms is even a part of how we describe our homes. When you start house hunting, you say to your real-estate agent, "We're looking for a three-bedroom, two-bath house."

British bathroom designer Edward Lewis pointed out that we spend one and a half years of our lives in bathrooms. He went on to say, "The bathroom is the one room in which we are able to finally switch off from all that is going on around us and simply be alone with our thoughts, and reflect on the day. A chance to relax and wash away life's little stresses, and above all, where inspiration strikes. It's an experience!"[3]

Keeping in mind the importance of the bathroom in our daily pattern, I can think of at least three benefits to a minimalist bathroom:

1. It's usually a relatively small space and yet is one where we spend a considerable amount of time. Clutter in a small space only seems like more clutter.

2. Bathrooms get dirty quickly—and not just dust, but grimy, sticky, gross stuff. A minimized bathroom is easier to clean, which makes using the room more enjoyable for everyone.

3. When we minimize here, we remove some stress in the morning from getting ready to meet the world. And, as Lewis said, we create a space that helps us wind down and relax at the end of the day when we're preparing for bedtime.

Your bathrooms have a greater significance to your family than their size would indicate, and you'll be glad when you've transformed them through decluttering.

ALL-NATURAL, ALL-PURPOSE CLEANER

1. Combine 1 teaspoon borax, $1/2$ teaspoon washing soda, and 1 teaspoon liquid Castile soap in a spray bottle.
2. Add 2 cups warm distilled water.
3. Add a few drops of the essential oils of your choice (such as lemon, lavender, or orange).
4. Put the spray top on the bottle and shake well.
5. Use on bathroom surfaces, kitchen counters, and elsewhere.
   —courtesy of Katie Wells, Wellness Mama[4]

READY-TO-GO LAUNDRY SOAP

1. Grate an unscented bar of soap (such as Dr. Bronner's or Ivory) until finely ground.
2. In a large bowl, mix bar of grated soap, 1 cup washing soda, and 1 cup borax.
3. Store in a closed container.
4. Use between 2 tablespoons and $1/4$ cup per laundry load.
   —courtesy of Katie Wells, Wellness Mama[5]

★ STEP-BY-STEP MINIMIZING FOR YOUR BATHROOMS

As you go about minimizing your bathrooms, your approach may vary from one to another.

- For your master bathroom, if you live alone, you have to please only yourself with what you choose to minimize. But if you have a partner, you'd better consult him or her before decluttering this room. You're probably going to go for a combination of cleaning efficiency and spa-like peacefulness for this room.
- For a kids' bathroom, you probably want a room that is easy to use and reflects a little of the kids' personalities. Ask them for their input on what they want to keep or are willing to get rid of. Space can be tight in kids' bathrooms, so every item matters.
- For your powder room or guest bathroom, imagine what your guests would like to find there. Probably you want it to be simple, easy to clean, and ready at a moment's notice.

1. Sort Through Your Medicine Cabinet

All of us have someplace where we keep prescription medicines, over-the-counter remedies, and the like. It might be behind a mirror in the bathroom, on shelves in the linen closet, or in drawers under the bathroom counter. On average, US households spend $486 on prescription drugs and $338 on OTC products every year.[6] Our medicine storage space is filled with everything from pain relief pills, to bandages, to bottles of sunscreen, to throat lozenges, to antiseptic spray, to thermometers, to cotton balls, to antacids, to skin lotion, and more.

Wherever you store this stuff, pull it all out and methodically go through it.

- Safely dispose of any prescription meds you're no longer using. Find out the preferred methods for disposing of those drugs in your area. For example, some pharmacies take back unused medications.[7]

- Similarly, get rid of any OTC medications or other products that have expired.
- Regardless of expiration date, get rid of anything that seems like it has gone bad (changed color, smell, or taste).
- Make sure you're not mixing different products in the same container.
- Discard all unmarked containers.
- Test medical devices and eliminate any that no longer work.
- Get rid of all unnecessary duplicates and anything you know you'll never use.

With most minimized items in the house, I recommend donating, selling, and recycling as removal options. With medicine cabinet items, however, these are *not* good options. Get rid of these items completely.

Organize what's left from your medicine cabinet so you can find what you need quickly and will know when it's time to restock. Store the items in a safe place where young children and curious visitors won't get at them. If any products can be damaged by humidity, place them in a sealed container for protection. In fact, you may want to move the entire collection to a private area outside your bathroom so that environmental damage and unauthorized browsing aren't concerns at all.

2. Pare Down Your Beauty and Grooming Supplies

I don't know if it's more about vanity or marketing, but increasingly both men and women worldwide are buying products with the intention of making themselves look better.

GoodHousekeeping.com reported, "The average woman owns a whopping *40* makeup products. . . . Even more shocking: On average, women typically only use *five* of those 40 products, meaning we allow 87% of our collection to go to waste without regular use."[8]

A UK newspaper reported 300 percent growth in sales of men's grooming products in 2015. It further said, "The top 10 boom markets for men's toiletries since 2010 include Brazil, South Korea, the US, Germany, India and, yes, the UK. In China, another of that top 10, year-on-year growth has exceeded 20 per cent over the same period."[9]

To minimize your beauty products, start by taking all of them out of the cabinets or drawers where you store them.

- Group things by kind, both *beauty tools* (styling irons, micro-dermabrasion devices, shavers, hairbrushes, manicure kits, and so on) and *beauty products* (eyeliners, foundation, hair sprays, antiaging lotions, perfumes, aftershave, and the rest). Respectively, these are your beauty-aid durable goods and consumables.
- Eliminate unnecessary duplicates.
- Throw out anything that's broken or old. Although cosmetics don't usually carry expiration dates, using makeup—especially eye makeup—too long can carry health risks.
- Get rid of items you don't use, such as an eyebrow pencil that is darker than your hair or a cologne whose scent you don't care for.
- Pare down the number of lipstick shades you keep on hand.
- Favor cosmetics that can be used for more than one purpose. For example, some foundations can also be used as primers and concealers.

A few beauty and grooming products are toxic and should be disposed of in an environmentally responsible way. For example, the experts recommend that nail polish be treated as hazardous waste.

When you're done minimizing, wash your storage containers and organize what you're going to keep.

3. Make Kids' Bathrooms Age and Stage Appropriate

As kids grow up, they need different products in their bathroom. A girl, for instance, might go from keeping a lot of plastic hair accessories and scented soap in the bathroom, to wanting tween-styled hair products and inexpensive jewelry, to wanting the same kinds of makeup Mom uses. Just as their clothing needs change so rapidly that it's surprising to us grown-ups, so their bathroom needs change as well. Yet sometimes we store things in kids' bathrooms long after they are no longer being used.

Your home should be the antidote to stress. Not the cause of it.—Peter Walsh #minimalisthome

---

If you have kids, go through their bathrooms with their help and remove any unnecessary items, especially things they don't need or want anymore. For example, if your son is too old for bath toys, get rid of them. Sometimes we get so used to seeing things in the bathroom that we forget we no longer need them.

Your kids will appreciate the fact that the bathroom-cleaning chore will be easier for them as soon as there is less clutter—even if they never mention it.

4. Reduce Your Bathroom Cleaning Products to the Basics

The bathroom is one of the rooms in the house where we tend to store some of our cleaning supplies. Take all these out of your bathroom and decide which ones you really need. A few are obvious—you're probably going to want to have toilet bowl cleaner and glass cleaner, for example. But see how few products you can keep on hand and still get the cleaning job done.

Marketers often try to sell us cleaning products by touting their targeted purposes, but a few basic cleaners may be all you really need. If you've got some specialized cleaners in your bathroom, test them. Use them as directed and see if they do a better job for you than an all-purpose cleaner. If not, you don't need them. Gimmicky products are usually too good to be true and just end up cluttering our space.

If you've got the DIY spirit, you may want to create your own simple cleaners. By doing this, you will save money, will know exactly what chemicals you're using around your house, and can make more of the solution whenever you need it.

5. Reduce the Number of Your Towels

Towels are slow to wear out, and so over time we tend to accumulate a lot of them. Go through your selection of bath towels, hand towels, and washcloths. How many do you really need? Minimize to that level and get rid of the rest. Reducing the diversity of the styles and colors of your bathroom linen gives the room a cleaner look.

Here's a tip: If you keep smaller towels, they'll take up less space in your laundry. The largest bath towels are actually called *bath sheets*. Do you really need a sheet to dry off with?

6. Clear Off the Countertops

The most visible clutter in your bathroom is probably on the countertop. Maybe you've got an electric toothbrush sitting there at the ready. Maybe you left a hairbrush lying on its back. Is the toothpaste tube oozing goo? Is that a plugged-in blow-dryer sitting dangerously beside the sink? Oops!

A part of the problem with counter clutter may be that you've chosen to leave things on the counter because it seems more efficient to have them at hand. Here is the convenience fallacy again. It actually takes very little time to remove a toiletry or beauty item from a drawer and put it back after you're done with it. And keeping so many things out not only creates visual distraction but also makes it harder to root through everything that's clustered on the countertop.

If you've gotten rid of things in your drawers and cabinets and under the sink, you can put more things away and keep that counter beautifully clean.

7. Declutter Around the Bathtub and in the Shower

Soap, shampoo, conditioner, bath salts, bath foam, oils, sponges, candles—the rims and shelves around a tub or shower tend to get cluttered with many items like these. Go through your collection and see what you can get rid of or put away more neatly. You'll like having the extra space and the ease of cleaning.

The number of products we need to clean our bodies is really very small.

In a day and age when we do less manual labor and therefore sweat less than earlier generations, it's especially ironic that we buy so many more bathing products. Don't make cleaning your body overcomplicated and clutter up your precious space.

WHAT TO DO WITH CONSUMABLES

Consumable goods are products that consumers use as needed, over a relatively short period of time, until the supply is gone or replenished. These are the opposite of *durable goods*—things that last and that we tend to keep around for a long time.

We need some consumables—just not as many as advertisers try to sell to us. And often we keep more consumables on hand than we will use in a short period of time, thus making our clutter problem worse.

When facing a stock of consumables in your home, ask yourself these questions:

1. Do I have room to store these items out of sight, or are they in plain view and distracting to me?
2. If I keep all these products, how quickly will I go through them?
3. Do I have the kind of personality that will enable me to use them to the end of the pile? Or is my personality type such that I will forget about the supplies and buy more even though the first pile hasn't run out?
4. How accessible are the consumables when I do run out? (If they're easy to replace, you don't need to keep as many around.)
5. Do I have unopened bottles of cleaners and packages of supplies that I could donate, or are they all partially used?

Simple Is Beautiful

Throwing out unwanted cosmetics or getting rid of the extra blow-dryer—these kinds of actions might not seem like a big deal to you. Well, let me tell you—minimizing your bathroom is a countercultural act!

Ask yourself why we tend to have so much bathroom stuff in the first place. Marketers are appealing to our base fears and insecurities, suggesting that we'll repel others with our body odors and grungy looks. On the other hand, they want us to think that if we use their products, we'll be beautiful, sexy, and alluring.

Katherine Ashenburg, author of *The Dirt on Clean,* put it in historical perspective:

> Advertising created a morbid worry about "offending," and more soaps, deodorants and mouthwashes (use Listerine and you would avoid the fate of being "often a bridesmaid but never a bride") rushed in to assuage that anxiety. . . .
>
> In the 21st-century, . . . little has changed. Soaps proliferate, the "intimate hygiene" products multiply and our goal seems to be to eradicate every natural smell from our bodies and then apply tropical aromas like vanilla and melon.[10]

The average US citizen spends $325 annually on toiletries. We're talking about a $35 billion industry.[11] So there's a lot of money at stake. Is it possible we're going too far, maybe just a little bit?

Now, let's be clear about this: I'm all for cleanliness. And there's nothing wrong with highlighting our natural beauty. But there is plenty of room for us to become more savvy about consumerism in this area, as in any other. Buying too many personal cleaning and beauty supplies is expensive and clutters up our homes—and it's just not necessary. Our time and money can be better spent in other places.

Overusing body cleaning products can even be harmful to us. Washing removes natural oils and can leave skin irritated. Aluminum in some antiperspirants and chemicals in deodorants can be toxic. Antibacterial washes remove good bacteria from the skin and can reduce our immunity to some diseases.[12]

At the same time we're making over our bathrooms, let's make over our attitudes toward cleanliness and beauty. How many of the items in our bathrooms are the result of external societal pressure urging us to conform? It is liberating to remove this thinking from our minds and those products from our bathrooms. Let's stick with the simple, the natural, and the necessary

---

Inspiration

THE ANSWER WAS LESS

I have lusted after a spa-like, Pinterest-worthy bathroom ever since I had my own home. The idea of getting that spa feeling inside my own four walls was too tempting to resist.

For years, I'd peppered the room with odds and ends here and there in an attempt to create that elusive mood I was after. I collected high-end products and pretty much anything that promised to transform me into a Victoria's Secret model. My bathroom was jam-packed with half-used bottles, samples, and unwanted gift sets.

It wasn't until I decluttered my bathroom that I finally got that calm, relaxing feeling I'd been trying to create. The answer to my problem, unbeknownst to me at the time, had always been less. It never occurred to me that the way to create a retreat-like space with a luxurious feel to it was to fill it with less stuff, rather than more.

—Jessica Rose Williams, England

instead. There's no need to look at your bathroom as a workshop for remaking your outer appearance into an image you think others will approve of.

An improved attitude can help you maintain the minimalism of your bathrooms. If you're more rational about cleanliness and beauty, you'll be less tempted to overaccumulate and overuse personal cleaning and beauty supplies. You can let go of society's bias about what you must look like at the same time you let go of society's idea of how much you must own.

Now, *that's* beautiful!

★ STEP-BY-STEP MINIMIZING FOR YOUR LAUNDRY ROOM

Before we finish thinking about how to minimize the cleaning spaces in the home, let's not forget to address the laundry room.

This room is perhaps the most purely utilitarian room in the house. Normally it's got one purpose—to serve as a cleaning station for our laundry. So in minimizing it we should strive to make it as efficient as possible for its simple use.

1. Remove Things That Don't Belong

When a laundry room becomes a storage area for all sorts of unneeded possessions that have nothing to do with laundry, it becomes less efficient and less enjoyable to work in. If you look about your laundry room and find objects that have migrated in for no good reason, ask yourself where else in the home they belong and move them there. Or maybe you can do without them altogether.

2. Take Down Unhelpful Decorations

I don't feel a need to decorate our laundry room with wall pictures or anything of that sort, but if you want to decorate yours, just make sure the decorations aren't overdone—that only produces a cluttery effect. Also make sure they aren't presenting a damaging message.

I know a woman with a sign in her laundry room that says, "It's tough living in the fast lane when you're married to a speed bump." Cute, clever, and worth a chuckle, I suppose. But I often wonder how reading that sign every day might affect her approach to her marriage, even in small ways.

We might put up cynical or critical messages in any room of the house, but somehow these seem to be particularly prevalent in laundry rooms.

I get the humor. I really do. But if we're going to be putting up signs on our walls in our own homes, shouldn't they be encouraging us to do our work well and selflessly instead?

3. Remove Unnecessary Laundry Products, Tools, and Accessories

The market is filled with laundry products—pretreatment and stain removers, bleach, laundry detergents (liquid, powder, or pod; for white clothes, dark clothes, or bright clothes), color catchers, fabric softeners and fabric conditioners, fabric deodorizers, and starch and antistatic spray. You don't need all of these. Just keep the basics that you'll use over and over.

In our house, we keep one stain remover, one laundry detergent that is suited for our washer type and works with all colors of clothing, one bottle of bleach, and one box of dryer sheets. That's it. (And we could probably get rid of the dryer sheets.)

In addition to laundry cleaning products, some of us have also accumulated laundry tools and accessories of different kinds, such as a lint brush or lint roller, clothesline, clothespins, iron, ironing board, drying rack, hampers or baskets, hangers, and washer bags. Got any of these that you can do without? Maybe you can open up space, allowing you to move about more freely in your laundry room and be more comfortable as you do the work the room is intended for.

4. Put the Supplies You Need Where They're Easy to Reach

Once you're down to just the supplies you're going to use with your laundry, organize them neatly and logically. They might be in boxes, bins, or cabinets. Or on shelves.

The laundry room is one of the few areas in the house where I think it can make sense to keep things out in the open. Usually I advocate keeping smaller items hidden in drawers and cabinets to give a room a cleaner look, but since the whole laundry room is typically closed off from regular view, it's not so important to hide the individual items. That's why, in our house, we have a shelf above our washer and dryer where we keep the laundry products within easy reach. Here, convenience is no fallacy.

Nobility in Your Humblest Rooms

The bathroom and the laundry room may be humble, utilitarian spaces, but let me point out a simple fact you may have overlooked: they can also be noble places.

If you're cleaning yourself and attending to your own grooming regularly (without overemphasizing appearance), you're making an effort to present yourself well to the world.

If you're taking the time to relax in a bubble bath periodically, you're recognizing that life is not all about activity and achievement and that there are suitable times to de-stress and meditate.

> It's better to have extra time on your hands and extra money in your pocket than extra stuff in your closet. #minimalisthome

If you're monitoring your weight on a scale or taking vitamin supplements kept in your bathroom, you're pursuing the value of health.

If you're storing medical supplies that you can grab when a child wakes up sick in the night, you're prepared to bring relief.

If you're bathing an infant, or perhaps a disabled spouse or elderly parent, you're giving comfort while serving a basic human need.

If you're teaching and modeling a simple approach to health and beauty for your kids, you're helping to start them out well in life.

If you're going through the routine of washing your family's clothes week in and week out, they may not thank you but they owe you.

Let *me* say it: thank you for caring and thank you for making the most of these spaces in your house by keeping them tidy and uncluttered.

Minimizing Checklist

How will you know when you've cleared out enough clutter and excess from your bathrooms and laundry room? Ask yourself these questions:

For the bathrooms . . .

- ☐ Have I done my best to create spaces where my family can relax and "wash away life's little stresses"?
- ☐ Have I removed all the things from the bathrooms that we do not need?
- ☐ Are the countertops clean and tidy?
- ☐ Are the drawers and cabinets organized, allowing needed products to be accessed quickly?
- ☐ Do these spaces empower my family members and me with confidence to feel good about ourselves and the day ahead?

For the laundry room . . .

- ☐ Have I arranged this room in an efficient way?
- ☐ Do the surroundings in this space encourage me to serve my family with love and selflessness?

The Heart of the Home

Decluttering the Kitchen and Dining Room

As I mentioned earlier, the nonprofit that my wife and I started with our minimalism dividend is an orphanage alternative called The Hope Effect, where orphaned children can live in a home that mimics the family. When I engaged an architect to design the first structure for this nonprofit, I told her, "We want to communicate security and community even in the way we design our homes. Everything has to be intentional."

The result was a home with a large kitchen and a dedicated eating area. "These are the places families grow closest together," our architect said.

So true, isn't it?

When I first became minimalist, I investigated what other minimalists were choosing to eliminate and keep. One thing I noticed was that some people kept very little related to cooking and eating. I remember one couple who owned only two plates and two forks!

I knew right away this extreme wasn't for us. For sure, we would get rid of a lot of things from our kitchen and dining room, but I didn't want to eliminate so much that we lost the purpose of cooking and eating as a family. In fact, I wanted our minimizing to *enhance* the joy of being together with others around food—both for us as a family and for the people we invite into our home.

At the time, we had three different groups from our church who would come over to meet in our home regularly, and I was also meeting with two engaged couples at our home to provide premarital counseling. We wanted to be able to host these people and others for informal meals. To do that, we wanted to keep a dining table and some chairs as well as some utensils for cooking food and plates to put the food on.

Meal hospitality is still a priority for us, along with serving nutritious dinners for our family of four, so these values have guided our minimalism in the kitchen and dining room.

Nevertheless, I'm not sure I can quite express what is so basic, so *right*, so utterly *human* about cooking and eating together. As far back as you can go in history, you find human beings gathering around tables (or just open fires) for

---

Minimalist Home Value

HOSPITALITY

Mingling in the kitchen during food preparation and then moving to the dining area to sit down and enjoy the results—that's got to be one of the greatest ways to experience the simple joy of living. And because they're uncluttered and ready to be useful to us, a minimized kitchen and dining room help us foster the inner life of the home: the relationships within it.

My next-door neighbor recently told me a story of having a married couple over for dinner. This couple had been feuding with one another for some time. "They brought their divorce papers with them, ready to sign," the wife from next door told me. "By the end of the meal, they had put them away, at least for the moment." This was an intentional use of their dining room to play a healing role in their friends' lives.

The same day I heard that story, our daughter's friend was over

the purpose of eating together. Offering food and water is an instinctive act of courtesy in almost every culture around the world. In the Bible and Jewish-Christian tradition, breaking bread together is perhaps both the humblest and the most meaningful reflection of unity.

Ayelet Fishbach, a professor of behavioral science at the University of Chicago, said, "Food really connects people. Food is about bringing something into the body. And to eat the same food suggests that we are both willing to bring the same thing into our bodies. People just feel closer to people who are eating the same food as they do. And then trust, cooperation, these are just consequences of feeling close to someone."[1]

In our modern homes, the kitchen so often seems to be the place for spontaneous, informal gatherings. There we can talk together while keeping our

---

for a playdate, and because it was getting late, we invited her to stay for dinner. This friend is from a dysfunctional home, and her young face is beginning to show the pain of it. For this one evening meal, around our dining room table, she got to see how a healthy family interacts with one another. We didn't plan it, and obviously this one meal won't solve all her problems at home, but maybe in a small way our interaction that evening will help her in the future when she has a family of her own.

And then there's the hospitality we don't always think of as hospitality: the kindness and attention we pay to our own loved ones, whom we live with every day. Making a meal—and making time to share it around the family table—is an act of love toward those we'd miss desperately if they weren't living in our homes and eating at our tables anymore. A meal together is an act of love.

A minimalist home can be a home that's always primed to say, "Welcome."

hands busy in an atmosphere of warmth emanating from the oven, rising steam, enticing odors, cheerful clinks and clatter, and the natural beauty of fruits and vegetables, all seasoned with the sauce of anticipation about the meal to come.

A dining area is where we sit down to share the food, and to share the time that it takes to eat the food, with others. Couples catch up with each other at the dinner table. Families review their days, take care of family "business," and joke around the meal. At the table, guests may be welcomed in an even friendlier way than is possible in the living room. There's a kind of everyday ritual about eating together that is reassuring in its repetition. Holiday meals are our domestic pageantry.

Therefore, it's a great idea to clog up our kitchens with every gadget that's been advertised, to the point where we get frustrated looking for what we need, with the countertops meanwhile being messy, cluttered, and ugly. Right? And to crowd our dining room with so much furniture and stores of tableware options that it's uncomfortable to eat there. Right? Obviously not. These spaces serve their purposes so much better when they are kept simple and inviting, letting us focus on the practical cooking tasks before us and the relational joys of sharing food together.

With these two rooms, we're getting to more difficult areas to minimize, because they (the kitchen in particular) tend to collect all sorts of items that we're going to have to sort through when we minimize. But you'll find that uncluttering the kitchen and dining area in your home is so worth it because here you are uncluttering the heart of the home!

Creating Your Home's Culture in the Kitchen

There is something refreshing and life giving about a clean, uncluttered kitchen. In fact, it is one of my favorite benefits of a minimalist lifestyle. It sets the tone and culture for the home. It communicates calm and order. It promotes opportunity and possibility. It saves time and ensures cleanliness.

Yet it is one of the more difficult places in the home to keep uncluttered. There are several reasons for this being such a difficult space to minimize:

- The kitchen is usually located in a high-traffic area of the home.
- The purpose of the room requires messes to be made during its use.
- The kitchen is often used as a collection area for odds and ends (such as mail).

Kitchen gear is one of the areas where marketers have gone overboard in promoting stuff we supposedly need. (Actually, they "need" our hard-earned dollars.) Here our culture of excess is clearly on display.

So, how crowded are our kitchens? One consumer expert wrote,

In the United States, the typical large kitchen in 2004 contained 330 different and a total of 1,019 items. Even a small one had a total of 655 items—three times as many as in 1948. Waffle irons, blenders, grapefruit spoons and espresso cups are all competing for space. Countertops have consequently been getting bigger, as have drawers. The ideal of the eat-in kitchen, where hosts can demonstrate their culinary skills, has added recipe books and specialized equipment, even if these are rarely used.[2]

The proliferation of kitchen appliances is one sign of the extremes of accumulation to which we've gone. The number of appliances (including but not restricted to kitchen appliances) purchased around the world has increased steadily, growing by 35 percent in just the decade spanning 2006 and 2016.[3] Today, about a quarter of US homes have two refrigerators—the most popular home appliance.[4]

If we were getting good use out of all these appliances, we could at least make a case for keeping them. But is that really what's happening? Research in the United Kingdom showed that two out of three households surveyed owned appliances that had been used an average of six times, while 10 percent of appliances had never been touched after being purchased. Britons own an estimated 123 million bread makers, coffee machines, food processors, and other kitchen devices that gather dust on the shelves.[5]

When you think about your own kitchen, what kinds of clutter come to mind? Are you one of those people who has been seduced by shiny gadgets or specialized tools that aren't really necessary? Do you have a lot of duplicates from when you got married and merged your kitchen supplies with your spouse's? Have you accumulated an extensive cookbook collection even though you use only one or two favorite cookbooks regularly?

If your kitchen is anything like most people's, you can get rid of a *lot* there.

Think about what you want your kitchen to accomplish for you. Is it to enable you to cook tasty, healthy meals for your family without too much fuss? Is it to be easy to keep clean so it offers you a sense of peace and doesn't waste your time? Is it to serve as a comfortable space for family or friends to keep you company as you cook?

Be clear on these goals, and use them to guide you as you ask *Do I really need this?* and minimize your kitchen.

At this point, if you fancy yourself a chef, have spurts where cooking provides you comfort like nothing else, or just love good food, you may be nervous that minimizing your kitchen is going to ruin your workshop for culinary creation. Relax! It's like minimizing anywhere else in the house—minimizing in the kitchen doesn't take away from you but rather gives. You can uncover what's been obscured about the joy of cooking by removing the excess objects from your kitchen work space. Minimalism will help you fall back in love with cooking—or maybe even fall in love for the first time.

Now You're Cookin'

From the start of our minimalism journey, I dreaded the day we would get to the kitchen. So many gadgets in so many drawers and so many pots, pans, and bowls on so many shelves—I had no idea where to start. But help arrived one afternoon while I was cruising the internet.

I found an article in the *New York Times* titled "A No-Frills Kitchen Still Cooks" in which professional chef Mark Bittman told how he decked out an entire kitchen for about $300 including every cooking utensil someone would need to cook like a pro. Not only did he list every utensil you'd need to create even the most elegant of dishes, but he listed exactly how much to spend on it.

ALL YOU NEED IN THE KITCHEN

Mark Bittman is the *New York Times*'s "minimalist cook" and author, whose books include: *How to Cook Everything*, *The VB6 Cookbook*, and *The Food Matters Cookbook*. Bittman says you can do virtually all the cooking you need to with just these cooking supplies.[6] Use this list as your guide when minimizing your kitchen:

- eight-inch, plastic-handle stainless alloy chef's knife
- instant-read thermometer
- three stainless steel bowls
- sturdy pair of tongs
- sturdy sheet pan
- plastic cutting board
- paring knife
- can opener
- vegetable peeler
- colander
- small, medium, and large cast-aluminum saucepans
- medium nonstick cast-aluminum pan
- large steep-sided, heavier-duty steel pan
- skimmer
- slotted spoon
- heat-resistant rubber spatula
- bread knife
- big whisk
- food processor
- salad spinner
- Microplane grater
- coffee and spice grinder
- blender
- knife sharpener

Throughout the piece, he promoted this philosophy: "It needs only to be functional, not prestigious, lavish or expensive."[7]

When the Saturday designated for minimizing our kitchen arrived, I set aside a significant part of the day for the project. I knew it would require intentional focus and energy. I was right, but the project did take less time than I had imagined.

Similar to what we had already done in other rooms, we pulled every item out of every drawer and cabinet and began sorting the contents into piles: keep, relocate, and discard. The discard pile was further subdivided into sell, recycle, and trash piles. With the help of the *New York Times* article, we created a list of every cooking or baking utensil we needed to keep. (It's a good strategy in any crowded part of the home. Rather than asking what you can remove from the area, start with an "essentials list"—and keep only those items.) It worked beautifully for us. By the time we were done, the kitchen no longer presented the clutter cavalcade it had before, and experience soon proved that we could create wonderful meals in it with no problem.

★ STEP-BY-STEP MINIMIZING FOR YOUR KITCHEN

Pick a time—maybe start first thing in the morning (that's what I did)—to minimize your kitchen when you have at least a couple of hours for the project. Make a cup of coffee or turn on some music to put yourself at ease. Clean space on the counters to set out items. And then when you are ready to jump in with minimizing your kitchen, try these helpful principles:

1. Relocate Anything That Does Not Belong in the Kitchen

Kitchens are notorious for becoming collection areas for odds and ends. Unintentionally, the kitchen becomes a storing place for mail, kids' homework, purses, keys, and all that stuff in the infamous junk drawer.

Identify a new "home" within the home for each out-of-place item and move it there. As you're doing so, tell yourself that you're going to change the culture in your home that allowed all that clutter to stay there in the kitchen in the first place. Think of your kitchen as a department store customer service area—items may enter there, but they shouldn't stay.

2. Notice Physical Boundaries

You will notice physical boundaries all over your kitchen—I'm talking about things like drawers and cabinets that provide defined, limited spaces for storage. Too often, we frown at these limitations and stubbornly shove as much as we can inside these spaces. But one of the biggest causes of clutter in our homes is our tendency to put too much stuff in too small a space, only to get upset the next time we have to rummage through it.

Rather than complaining about the physical boundaries in your kitchen,

---

LOVE THEM MULTITASKERS

Wherever in your home you have a collection of tools of some kind (shop tools, gardening tools, definitely kitchen tools), there's one strategy that can help you easily pare down the collection: favor multitaskers over unitaskers.

Multitaskers do many things, while unitaskers do only one. You probably have a lot of both kinds of tools in your kitchen.

From strawberry slicers and quesadilla makers to avocado preservers and the Amco One-Step Corn Kerneler (yes, it's real), unitaskers promise convenience but rarely deliver. Instead, they are costly and cumbersome. Few of them complete a task that can't be done just as well by a far more common kitchen tool, such as a knife or skillet.

Save space and promote simplicity in your tool collections by getting rid of as many unitaskers as you can.

see them as helpful guidelines for how much stuff to keep. And think about how to use them to the greatest potential.

3. Remove Duplicates and Little-Used Items

Evaluate all the items in your kitchen by asking yourself the same question you ask everywhere else in the home. It's not *Might I conceivably use it at some time?* It's *Do I need it?* If you've rarely or never used a tool, bowl, or storage container, then you know it's probably not really necessary to keep.

By the way, I recommend you keep a set of plastic food containers that have lids that nest together and discard the others.

4. Give Every Item a Proper Home

Designate drawers for silverware and utensils; cupboards for plates, containers, pots and pans, and small appliances; and closets or shelves for food and larger, less-used appliances. After evaluating your physical boundaries and thinning out your kitchen possessions, you'll find this is easier than you think.

5. Clear the Counters

If your counters are routinely cluttered, there is a good chance you are storing many daily-use items there (toaster, coffee maker, teapot, can opener, spice rack, knife block, canister of wooden spoons, cutting board, and the like). You might also have out some of your standard baking ingredients, such as flour, sugar, cooking oil, and salt and pepper. Or maybe a large number of odds and ends. You've probably reasoned that leaving such things on the counters makes them easier to grab when you need them.

This is where the convenience fallacy, once again, comes into play.

The reality is that these items spend far more time as clutter than they do as needed instruments of food preparation. For example, if you make toast for breakfast, it will take you roughly three minutes to toast your bread. After that, the toaster will sit unused for the next twenty-three hours and fifty-seven minutes. Is leaving the toaster out where it's taking up counter space and creating visual distraction worth the few seconds you will save pulling it out when you're ready to drop your slice of bread into it in the morning? Think of all the times you've needed to move it to clean around or behind it or had to shuffle it about to create more working space on your counter.

Rather than allowing these appliances to take up counter space, find a home for them in an easily accessed part of the kitchen, such as inside a cabinet or on a shelf. In our home, for instance, we store the toaster, coffee maker, and teapot in a cupboard right next to the outlet. Getting them out when we need them and putting them away is a habit that takes us next to no time and leaves our counters wide open the rest of the day.

Your home minimalism can include everything, including the kitchen sink—literally! Put away any cleaning supplies (soap, scrubber, and so on) that currently clutter up the sink area.

6. Purge the Pantry

The whole point of a kitchen is consuming (food, that is), so you've got a lot of consumables in cabinets or in an adjacent closet used as a pantry.

- Pull out everything and group items by kind.
- Relocate whatever doesn't belong in the pantry.
- Clean the pantry.
- Put old and expired food items in the trash or compost.
- Begin putting foods back into the pantry in logical groupings, consolidating food packages where possible. As you're doing this, note where you need to reduce the amounts of certain foods by "eating through" your supplies or by donating unopened packages to a local food pantry.
- Organize items with bins, boxes, or see-through containers so you can see at a glance what you've got.
- Think about how you want to handle grocery shopping differently so you don't have so much food sitting around in your pantry.

Face to Face

Our homes today have many different kinds of eating spaces. Kitchen-counter overhang with bar stools. Breakfast nook or kitchen eat-in area. Formal dining room. Snack table in the family room or counter in a secondary kitchen in the basement. Patio or deck table adjacent to an outdoor grill. Backyard picnic table.

In the old days when many larger homes had domestic servants, the family ate in a formal dining room, while the servants ate in the kitchen. But very few homes have servants anymore, and so most families naturally prefer the convenience and coziness of eating in a dining area within or attached to the kitchen. Still, about two-thirds of homes do have separate dining rooms.[8]

Inspiration

HOT, BUTTERY SCONES

Something happened this morning that wouldn't have happened six weeks ago.

I was standing in my uncluttered kitchen waiting for my coffee (blessed coffee—it's the only thing that gets both my eyes pointing in the same direction in the morning), and my eyes traveled over my shiny counter. Only one thing rested on it: a large, beautiful, healthy Granny Smith apple. It was not supposed to be there (one of the kids must have left it there), so I automatically moved to put it away.

But wait! I was in my peaceful, newly minimized kitchen. So I got out my mixing bowl. I knew exactly where it was, and it was clean, and now there were only two of them (one big, one small). I didn't have to root through my utensil drawer for my pastry cutter, because it was right there. Same for my butter from my clean fridge and for my flour, which I had transferred to a handy place in a drawer.

How many and what kinds of eating spaces does your home have? What do they contain?

If you have a separate dining room, it may feature some of your largest pieces of furniture, perhaps including a dining table with extension leaf, a china cabinet or hutch, and a sideboard. These pieces take up a lot of space. I've been a guest at homes where there was so much furniture crowding the dining room that it was uncomfortable to get in and out of my seat. Hardly relaxing! Is your dining room furniture helping your mealtime hospitality or hindering it? If you got rid of some of the stuff you store in these pieces of furniture, maybe you wouldn't need them all.

Meanwhile, in your dining room, you may be storing a lot of stuff. You may have sturdy everyday tableware, fancy china that you keep for special

---

In fifteen minutes I had fresh apple cinnamon scones baking in the oven—*and* the kitchen had been returned to its pristine state. I unloaded the dishwasher while I waited for the scones to finish baking, then ate one hot from the oven with slivers of butter melting into it while I sat outside at my patio table.

I repeat: *This would not have happened before.* The counter would have been covered with clutter. I would not have bothered with cleaning the kitchen just to cook something on a whim. The flour would have inconveniently been in a bag somewhere. I would have had five different sets of cup measures, but don't ask me where. And finding the cinnamon? In *that* spice cupboard? It would be faster to walk to the grocery store and buy more cinnamon.

So this morning was an obvious sign to me that, yes, my minimizing efforts are paying off. Wow, is it ever nice!

—Cindy, Canada

occasions (and hope that the kids don't break), and birthday- or holiday-decorated sets of dishes. Likewise, you might have two or more sets of flatware (everyday and fancy), specialized or decorative serving dishes, and glassware or crystal: water glasses, wine glasses, dessert cups, and more. You may have different kinds of tablecloths and place mats, coasters, and table runners ready for your table-decorating whims. How about cloth napkins and napkin rings? Do you have more settings than you will ever likely use? Then there are the decorations—centerpieces suitable for different seasons and holidays, candles and candlesticks, vases, decorative bowls . . . what else?

> Just because you have the space doesn't mean you have to fill it with stuff. #minimalisthome

Now, some flexibility in setting a table can be useful. But do you really need all that stuff? If you're not using it much, isn't it just collecting dust and wasting space? If it sits idly for eleven-plus months of the year, is it really necessary?

Remember to think about what you're trying to accomplish in this room. I assume it's to create a comfortable, intimate, peaceful eating area for your family and any guests you may have over from time to time. You could be going beyond this purpose if you hold on to all your dining room items. For example, are you trying to impress others with all the fancy stuff you drag out only once or twice a year? Tim Chester said, "The focus of entertaining is impressing others; the focus of true hospitality is serving others."[9] Which focus does your dining room communicate?

Sitting down with others at a meal is a beautiful thing. After all, where else do we come face to face with a group of our loved ones at close range like this and with time to talk? But we don't need a lot of stuff to make the occasion memorable. Our dining room today contains three things: a table with eight chairs, one piece of wall art (a wedding gift from my sister), and two small decorative shelves. That's it for us. Your list will look a little different, but start thinking how you might minimize your dining room possessions until the space is doing *exactly* what you want it to and no more.

★ STEP-BY-STEP MINIMIZING FOR YOUR DINING ROOM

Simplifying your dining room hopefully won't be too hard for you (easier than the kitchen, anyway). And if you eat there three times a day, then three times a day you'll be able to enjoy the zone of peace you created there!

1. Relocate Items That Don't Belong in the Dining Room

Especially when we have a dining room that we don't use much, or that has furniture with a lot of cabinet space available, we are tempted to store things there that have nothing to do with eating meals. So stand in your dining room and look for items that you should move to other places in the house where they more naturally belong. Or if you're just storing certain items and not using them, why not get rid of them at once?

2. Clear the Dining Room Table

Like kitchen counters, many dining tables become depositories for mail, purses, keys, books, and other things that are in the process of going from one place to another. Sadly, if your table has as much of a clutter collection on it as some I've seen, using it for a meal may seem like more work than it's worth.

Put items away where they belong. Make the tabletop a clean, open space that says, "I'm ready for your next meal. Gather the loved ones and let's eat together!"

3. Reconsider Decorations

Take a look at the decorative items in your space. Which are the most meaningful to you and your family? Which are not? Is it time to take the antique glassware you inherited to a consignment store? Are there so many pieces of art, mottos, and other decorations on the walls that the room feels busy rather than beautiful? Do you really need all those plants, whether fake or real? Are the trinkets on the shelves more cluttery than captivating? Maybe the shelves themselves could go.

4. Remove Unneeded Furniture

Finally, look for large pieces of furniture that can be removed from the dining room to open up floor space. Maybe there's a side table or buffet or curio cabinet you really don't need. Make arrangements to part with it. This will open up a lot of space at once and complete your dining room minimizing.

Feeding the Soul

The kitchen and dining room form the heart of the home. Here is where our bodies and souls are fed simultaneously. We make these rooms more effective not by packing them with all the tools and decorations marketed for them but by relieving them of their burden of excess possessions. Let's let the people we love shine in these spaces, not all the unnecessary gadgets and tableware.

Picture your dream home. I bet it's not filled with clutter. #minimalisthome

---

The benefits of minimizing the kitchen and dining room far outweigh the effort it takes. Don't overlook the payback you'll get: When you're spending less time taking care of a cluttered kitchen, you'll have more time to make nutritious, delicious meals for your family and linger in conversation at the dinner table. When you're not overwhelming your family and guests with a bunch of decorations and fancy table settings, they'll be more comfortable at your meals.

Cooking and eating may be some of the basic human requirements for survival, but if we make room for loved ones in our kitchen and dining areas, we'll be exalting relationships by expanding everyone's opportunities for giving and receiving love.

Minimizing Checklist

How will you know when you've cleared out enough clutter and excess from your kitchen and dining room? Ask yourself these questions:

For the kitchen . . .

- ☐ Is my kitchen easy to maintain and keep clean? Does it promote safety?
- ☐ Is this a space I enjoy cooking in?
- ☐ Are the tools I use most frequently easy to access?
- ☐ Have I removed visual clutter from counters and surfaces?
- ☐ Does my kitchen promote healthy eating habits?
- ☐ Does this space encourage optimistic attitudes in the morning?

For the dining room . . .

- ☐ Does my dining room offer freedom to move about, rather than being cramped and cumbersome?
- ☐ Does my dining area offer opportunity for meals together as a family—a place where we can recap the day?
- ☐ Does my dining area encourage me to show hospitality to others?

8

Freeing the Mind

Decluttering the Home Office

For the first several years I was a minimalism advocate, I worked from my dining room table, putting away my laptop computer and any papers I was working with before the next mealtime came around. Working from home was such a simple way to be productive—and how great it was to be near my wife and to be so available for my kids while they were young! (Not to mention how convenient it was to leave my hair uncombed and lazily stroll to the table with a cup of coffee to work in the morning.) Nowadays I lease a small office because I find that putting some distance between myself and home helps me concentrate on my work better. But I still sometimes opt to work from the dining room table, and I still enjoy it when I do.

More and more people run businesses from home these days, whether it's a full-time gig or a side hustle. My next-door neighbor sells stuff on eBay. Another friend runs Facebook ads for businesses. I know others who sell motorcycle tires and "survivalist gear" (whatever that is) from their homes. An estimated 26 million Americans have a home office that they could legitimately claim a tax deduction for.[1]

A lot of people with more traditional jobs bring work home with them to finish up in the evenings. Also, an increasing number of people are making arrangements with their employers to do some of their work remotely (usually at home) during regular work hours, and they are doing so for longer periods of time during the week.[2] The digital revolution has helped to enable a work-place revolution, and lengthening urban commuting times make working at home that much more efficient and attractive. But it comes with its own clutter challenges.

Meanwhile, all of us have household accounts to keep up with. Bills to pay. Records to keep. Budgets to track. Investments to research. Taxes to compute. Schedules to organize.

HOW LONG TO KEEP RECORDS

The following are general guidelines. Rules may vary from area to area, and your individual circumstances may affect your choices. When in doubt, seek advice from an accountant, lawyer, or other expert.

For the rest of your life . . .

- birth and death certificates
- marriage licenses
- divorce decrees
- Social Security cards
- military discharge papers
- estate planning documents
- life insurance policies
- legal filings
- pension plan documents
- ID cards
- passports

For seven years . . .

- tax returns (or longer, if they contain inaccuracies)
- supporting tax documentation

Schoolkids need a place to do homework or want to borrow Mom's computer to do research.

I'm told some people use their computer to play games.

As a consequence of all this, most of us have a home office of some kind. It might be a separate room, or it might be a desk pushed in a corner of a bedroom, or it might be a dining room table, but regardless, we have someplace where we get work done at home. And the home office is one of those areas that

For a year or more . . .

- loan documents (until after the loan is paid off)
- vehicle titles (until after you sell the vehicle)
- house deeds (until after you sell the house)
- mortgage documents (until after you pay off the mortgage)
- investment purchase confirmations (until after you sell the investment)
- monthly bank and credit card statements (unless you can access them online)

For less than a year . . .

- ATM and bank deposit and withdrawal slips (until you reconcile with monthly statement)
- credit card receipts (until you reconcile with monthly statement)
- insurance policy (until the new one arrives)
- investment statement (until the new one arrives)
- Social Security statement (until the new one arrives)
- utility, cable, and cell phone bills (until you verify payment processed, or longer if you deduct these costs)

tend to accumulate a lot of small items and store unnecessary materials. Prime square footage, in other words, for a minimalism makeover.

Some of us have the idea that a messy, crowded office typifies a busy, productive worker. "My office is a mess, but I know where everything is" is a common mantra. Unfortunately, more often than not, a messy office typifies a disorganized, unfocused, stressed-out worker who is running behind and feels out of control. The good news is that this kind of discouraging work experience is not necessary in our home office if we'll minimize.

Marie Kenney, a friend of mine, expressed the view about office mess that I think most people share, if they're honest. "I cannot work or be creative in a cluttered environment," she said. "A clean and tidy, near-empty space allows me to think so much more clearly!"

When you free up space in your home office, you'll feel more at peace and be able to do your work more efficiently. And beyond that, I believe you'll also find that you've freed up your mind to think more clearly, make decisions better, and plan further ahead so that, instead of feeling you're at the mercy of the business and busyness of modern-day life, you'll be more proactive about your future. That's worth sorting through some files and throwing out some office supply duplicates, don't you think?

★ STEP-BY-STEP MINIMIZING FOR YOUR HOME OFFICE

Before minimizing your home office, clarify in your own mind how you want it to work. Are you running a business out of there? Is it just for processing the household accounts? Do you want it to be inspirational, encouraging creativity and dreaming, or would you rather keep it sparse and utilitarian? Is it a retreat where you like to read a book or sip a drink—more of a den than a mere office? Is it for the whole family or just the parents?

For many people, the home office can become a catchall space that is used for too many different activities. Clarify your purposes for your home office, and it will be easier to decide what to keep and what to get rid of.

1. Clear Out Storage Cabinets, Drawers, and Closets

The drawers and cabinets in our home offices have a way of collecting so much stuff that it almost looks like we're running our own business supply stores.

For one thing, there are the computer accessories: specialized cords that used to go to who-knows-what equipment, flash drives, an old printer you don't use anymore, ink for that old printer, manuals to current and past computer equipment. Get rid of anything obsolete or unnecessary. The manuals to your computer and printer are probably available online, so why not recycle the paper manuals? Using cloud backup these days? Then you can toss that old external hard drive. (Please recycle electronics waste responsibly.)

And then there are the office products. Here, you should distinguish between *equipment* (durable goods) and *supplies* (consumables).

- When it comes to equipment, you probably need only one of each type. One stapler, one tape dispenser, one pencil sharpener, for example. So here the duplicates rule comes into play—keep the best and get rid of the rest.

  Or maybe you don't even need some categories of equipment at all. When was the last time you used that three-hole puncher? Since you have a calculator app on your phone, can you get rid of that too?

- When it comes to consumable supplies—stationery, envelopes, file folders, labels, paper clips, Post-it Notes, pens, pencils, colored markers, tape rolls, staples, and so on—it might make more sense to keep a collection, because you're presuming you'll use them up over time. Often, however, we use up office supplies rather slowly. So consider the time frame: if you're not going to use up your supply in a year or so, maybe you have too many. If they're distracting to you, get rid of some of them. For the rest, store them neatly out of sight.

If you were to look in the drawers of my office, you would find one ream of printer paper, a small box of preprinted envelopes, a stack of marked-up Moleskine planners, and one manila folder that I use each day. I keep only three pens (one in my bag, one in my drawer, and one Sharpie that I take on trips to sign books with). Additionally, I keep a plastic box of financial records in my office. Other than that, I've got nothing in my office drawers. (Well, maybe a few snacks.)

You might have different needs for office equipment and supplies than I do, but I bet you don't need nearly as much as you've got stashed away in your office.

2. Reduce the Number of Books on Your Shelves

You may have bookshelves in more than one room in your house, such as your living room or bedroom. The home office is certainly a likely place for storing books. How do you decide which to keep and which to give away?

Easy enough. Let me suggest four categories for your books, regardless of which room you keep them in:

- Books you own but have never read and don't realistically expect to read. Don't hold on to them for "someday." Donate them today.
- Books you have read but will never go back to. Donate these too.
- Books that you have read and that have become influential in your life. Keep them. Or even better, lend them to someone else who might get just as much out of them as you have.
- Books you have already read and know you will want to return to. Of course, keep these.

Shelves looking better now?

3. Simplify the Walls

I'm not sure why, but home offices can be some of the most overdecorated spaces in the house.

Take a critical look at the walls of your home office. Are they crowded with photos, posters, or inspirational plaques? Do you have an "ego wall" of diplomas and certificates? Do you have some wall-attached shelving that's displaying a multitude of small objects? Get rid of anything that's more distracting than helpful. And while you're at it, maybe you can take down some of the shelves themselves or even a whiteboard or bulletin board you don't need.

4. Go Through Your Filing Cabinets

When faced with a piece of paper that you think you need or that you're not sure you need, it's so easy to decide, *I'll just file it.* Problem solved, right? The paper is out of sight but available if you want to return to it.

Actually, problem created because this tendency leads us to save far more paper than we need. Most of our papers we don't need at all or we could store in a different format, and if we ever do need to return to a piece of paper, it can be hard to find amid all the excess.

> The first step in crafting the life you want is to get rid of everything you don't. #minimalisthome

To file papers, you need hanging file folders, labels, and the file cabinets themselves. It all takes up space. Also, it leaves the disquieting realization in your mind that there's a whole bunch of paper stored inside those sliding drawers and that some time or other you're going to have to face it all again.

That time is now. Go through the papers and clear out what you don't need. You can read more about this important topic under "How Long to Keep Records" on pages 126–127.

5. Remove Furniture and Accessories You No Longer Need

Have you eliminated enough old or unnecessary files so that you can now get rid of that ugly metal file cabinet in the corner? Great! Do it.

Can you dispense with the credenza that takes up so much floor space? Can you eliminate a bookshelf unit? Can you reduce to just two chairs—one at the desk and one for a visitor? Go ahead. Maybe you have a local donation

center or used office furniture store that would be glad to take these pieces off
your hands.

While you're at it, can you remove any office accessories, such as a TV,
music player, lamp, minifridge, clock, or magazine rack?

With bigger pieces gone, your office should really be feeling more spacious
and peaceful now.

6. Give Yourself the Gift of a Wide-Open Desktop

The desktop is an area where the convenience fallacy can run wild. Is your
desktop cluttered with things you think you need to have at hand? What's
there? A printer? Phone? Pens and pencils? Scraps of paper with scribbled messages to yourself? A clock? Photos? Potted plants? Overflowing paper tray?
Fidgets? Goofy souvenirs? Coffee mug or water bottle?

Be bold in getting rid of all you can do without. Do you really need the
clock, since you always have the time on your computer and phone anyway?
You can write with only one pen or pencil at a time, so isn't that enough to have
at hand? If you're done with the papers, put them in your recycling bin. Plants
are great—just not too many.

If you can't get rid of something, can you relocate it to a place where it
belongs better? (Coffee mug in the kitchen, please.) Or can you store it away in
the drawers or on the shelves you've already minimized?

When you're satisfied that what's on your desktop is only what you really
need or really, really want at hand when you're working, arrange this stuff
neatly and wipe down the desktop. Then enjoy the wide-open vista of creativity
it presents.

Be a Paper Tiger

Paper is one of the biggest clutter culprits in the home, especially in the home
office. Newspapers, advertisement flyers, and other pieces of mail often end up
here. We create or bring home stacks of paper for work projects. We keep finan-

cial statements from banks and investment companies, correspondence from insurance companies and medical providers, vehicle records, donation receipts from nonprofits, previous years' tax forms, and who knows what else. They're stuffed in manila file folders, hanging in file cabinets, pierced in binder notebooks, piled loose leaf in stacks, and left yellowing in boxes.

A single piece of paper doesn't take up much space, but the thousands, or even tens of thousands, of pieces that we keep can get surprisingly space consuming. And more than that, they contain so much diverse information and are so hard to organize that their very existence in quantity creates a mental burden far out of proportion to their physical size.

Minimalist Home Value

WORK

One of the minimalist home values in the bedroom chapter was *rest*. Another minimalist home value is seemingly the opposite: *work*. But not frantic work. Peaceful, purposeful work. Efficient, effective work.

Work—whether it's paid work or volunteer work or creative work—is a big part of what we're here for on this earth. It builds the dignity of self-reliance in us at the same time it calls forth our generous instincts by putting us in a position where we can help others.

In all areas, minimalism maximizes our potential. And that's especially so for minimizing the home office—it turns this space into an environment that helps us get more and better work done with less stress. It might actually transform the legacy we leave.

Work is a four-letter word to many, but it's not supposed to be like that. Remember the excitement of starting your career? Let minimalism help you fall back in love with work.

Be a paper tiger. Attack your paper and don't give up until the only papers left in your home office are the ones that must be there and you know exactly where to put your hands on them.

When you're minimizing the backlog of paper in your office, keep the following three categories in mind because they should encompass all the paper you're dealing with:

1. paper you must keep (at least for now)
2. paper you can get rid of
3. paper you can convert to digital storage

About the paper purge survivors

You may have a lot of paper left over from work projects you've completed and you can likely get rid of it, but you'll probably want to keep paperwork pertaining to your current project.

You don't need all those tests and book reports your kids' teachers sent home in past years, but you may want to keep a few that are special.

You don't need those receipts from 2006, but you may want to keep this year's receipts.

When you're asking yourself the *Do I really need this?* question about your papers, be tough minded in answering it because most of the time the answer should be no. But when it *is* yes, then keep it in good conscience, put it where it belongs, and make sure it's labeled so that you can find it again later. (You'll find that keeping only a minimal amount of paper makes organizing it much easier.) Use a fireproof safe or a safe-deposit box for the really important papers.

To the recycling bin

Once you have a stack of old records or other papers you don't need any more, toss them in the recycling bin. Far better a full recycling bin (for now) than files and cabinets overflowing with paper that's no longer of any use to you.

There are a lot of gadgets sold for home offices that aren't really necessary, but one that can actually be an aid to minimalism is a paper shredder. Use yours to shred any documents that have revealing financial or other sensitive information on them. If you have a great deal of paper to shred, you may want to use the services of a professional paper shredding company. Of course, if it's just a little bit or shredding that needs to happen in your office, choose to shred by hand—that's what I do.

From paper into pixels

There are going to be a lot of papers that you don't need in physical form but whose information it wouldn't be wise to get rid of yet. The easiest solution is to scan them into PDF documents that you store on your computer, then shred or recycle the paper originals. When they're in digital form, they're not taking up space in your office and they're easy to search for when you need them and easy to send by email to someone else. If in the future you decide you don't need them even in digital form, you can delete them with a click.

Remember these tips:

- Be sure to use a good file-naming system so you can find the document you want when searching.
- Be sure to back up your documents in at least one place, or better yet two.
- For documents with sensitive information, consider using password protection.

If you haven't tried this solution, I believe you'll find it surprisingly easy to scan a large number of documents quickly. If you have a scanner, a scan app on your phone, or a multifunction printer that scans, then you can do it yourself. If you don't have a scanner or don't want to take the time to do this work yourself, there are companies that will do it for you. Go online and search for "document conversion services." There are even some services that will allow you to rent commercial-grade scanners for a short time.

Digital Clutter

Digitizing information is a great way to reduce the need for paper in the home office. You can also save space in your home by scanning photo prints or burning old CDs or DVDs you own to your computer and then storing the originals out of sight.

In general, the digital revolution has been a huge boost to the minimalist movement—a beautiful thing, since it has come just as our society's material accumulation problem has reached critical dimensions. But that doesn't mean our digital devices—desktop or laptop computer, tablet, smartphone— wouldn't benefit from being minimized themselves. They, too, can accumulate clutter. And digital clutter is still clutter. It can also be distracting.

It feels better to do stuff than to have stuff. #minimalisthome

---

The UK's Craig Link, self-proclaimed "digital minimalist," came to minimalism the way many of us do. He was buying without satisfaction, eating to the damage of his health, and using his spare time to feed his TV and video game addictions—until finally he realized that he needed to radically simplify his life. He even extended his minimalism to his beloved technology. Craig said,

> It was only after I was able to simplify my life, that I realised just how urgently we need minimalism in this day and age. In fact, it may be more relevant and more important today than any other time in history.
>
> Some people love seeing technology evolve and others resent it. Either way, the reality is that it's not going away any time soon just as it is never truly finished.
>
> But as a technology enthusiast, I believe that if used in line with

the principles of minimalism, that computers, smartphones and digitisation can all help turn a complex life into a simple one.[3]

Maybe you don't need as many devices as you have. Maybe you kept your old notebook computer when you bought your new one—time to get rid of the old one. Maybe you don't use that tablet anymore—let it go. Maybe you listen to music from your phone now and don't need that old MP3 player anymore.

When you've got your devices down to the ideal number, use these tips to minimize them and prevent distractions:

- Remove as many icons from your desktop as possible.
- Uninstall software you don't need.
- Delete unneeded files from your Documents folder. (If you don't want to delete them completely, at least move them to an archive folder so they don't clutter your most-used folder anymore.)
- Develop a simple but logical folder structure so that you can find documents you want easily.
- Unsubscribe to blogs, email newsletters, and advertisements that no longer serve your interests.
- Delete internet bookmarks, cookies, and temporary internet files you no longer need.
- Delete apps you don't need, remembering that if you need them later, you can always download them again. Put only your most crucial apps (such as your calendar and phone) on your home screen. Put the rest in folders on your second screen.
- Turn off notifications, including social media push notifications and email audio alerts.
- Make sure your spam filters are working.
- Delete photos that are of poor quality or that you don't need.
- Delete unused music and movies.
- Subscribe to a password manager so that you don't have to keep track of a bunch of passwords.

Once you've minimized your devices, it should be easier to follow practices that keep you from using them too often.

A lot of people are obsessive in their use of technology. It's not entirely their own fault, since app developers go to a lot of trouble to make their content habit forming.[4] Did you know the typical cell phone user touches his phone more than two thousand times a day?[5] You can do better by creating boundaries between yourself and your technology. Check email and log on to your favorite social media sites just twice a day. Turn off your phone, put it out of reach, or put it on Do Not Disturb when you don't really need it or don't want others to interrupt you. Perhaps change your phone's screen to gray scale so that the screaming colors of your app icons don't tempt you too much. Don't presume you can keep up with everything in your Twitter feed, and don't feel you have to accept friend requests from everybody who wants to put her pet videos on your Facebook wall. Join fewer groups, play fewer games, poke fewer people, and chat less.

If you have kids, set boundaries for their use of the home office computer. Decide with them how much time they can spend and what they can do on the computer. Install filtering software to keep them from being exposed to explicit material.

Plotting Good

The benefits of a minimized home office appear on two levels. The first level has to do with being more efficient at your work (whether it's moneymaking work or household business)—finding what you need quickly, avoiding time wasters and attention distracters, and getting the job done. Minimizing your home office enables this room to do what it's supposed to do. That's pretty great.

The second level is even better! It's about opening up space to plan for a better future.

We talk about "getting on top of" our work. With a minimized home office, you can get—and stay—on top of whatever work you do there. And here's the thing: when you're on top of it, you can see more. You can foresee problems, dream of possibilities, and start taking steps to accomplish more.

Maybe after efficiently paying this month's bills, you can take some time to create that family budget you know you should have.

Maybe after quickly updating your family's schedule on your calendar

---

Inspiration

VANQUISHING THE DEBT MONSTER

When my wife and I got married, I had $50,000 in student loans, $17,000 in a car loan, and about $4,000 in credit cards. These are unfortunately typical for postcollege student debts. But that's a lot of debt to bring into a marriage.

My wife and I moved into an apartment and started working right away. After a year of marriage, we sat down and started budgeting. My wife was a minimalist before I was and often helped me rethink my desires for more things. I started to feel embarrassed about my credit card debt, knowing full well that she was right—I had spent a lot of money on things I didn't need.

Over the course of the next four and a half years, we put almost all our extra money into paying down our debt. Money that, in a previous life, I would have wasted on pointless things was now being directed toward an important pursuit. Because we chose minimalism, we had successfully paid off the student loan (our largest debt) just in time for our daughter's birth.

Minimalism allowed us to put the focus on getting rid of the debts we had, so now we can minister in our church and focus on our family without the distractions of meaningless debt or pointless items.

—Dan, USA

app, you'll be able to look ahead to next year's schedule and book a stay at that family resort you promised your kids.

Maybe after entering your home office on a Saturday morning and realizing you're totally caught up with your office chores, you can plan how to begin that part-time business you've been thinking about.

Along with all these possibilities, permit me to suggest one more: find a quiet moment to sit in your peaceful minimized office and dream about how you can make the world a better place. If minimalism is helping you save money, will you give some of that money away to a good cause? With more time available to you, what passions for service could you live out?

In other words, instead of using your office just to plot moneymaking or spending, use it to plot doing good. Make it mission central for your personal crusade to give back to society. Dream of what you can do with your newly freed-up life.

Minimizing Checklist

How will you know when you've cleared out enough clutter and excess from your home office? Ask yourself these questions:

- ☐ Does this space encourage me to focus on my work?
- ☐ Do the tools and supplies I have kept help me work better, or are they getting in the way of it?
- ☐ Does this space invite me to enjoy the work I do?
- ☐ Are my paper files organized in a way that makes sense to me?
- ☐ Is this work space convenient and efficient for each person I share it with?
- ☐ Does the technology around me solve problems or only contribute to them?
- ☐ Is this space easy to maintain? Have I left enough room in cabinets and drawers to put things away at the end of the day?

Unburdening Yourself of the Past

Decluttering the Storage and Hobby Areas and the Toy Room

Never in history have human beings had so much stuff inside their houses. One estimate puts the number of items inside the average American home at three hundred thousand.[1] Even if a home has only a half or a third as many as that, it's still an incredible number, isn't it? When I tell you to touch every item you're considering eliminating, that's a lot of items to touch (but you'll be glad you did). These possessions are spread all over the home, but a disproportionately large number of them are in storage areas within the home: an attic, a basement, a storage closet, or whatever it might be.

For the most part, these items in storage aren't consumables. They're durable goods that we don't use or even look at very often—and that's a clue right there that many of them are candidates for minimizing. If a possession fails the *Do I need this?* test and yet we hold on to it anyway, we've got a problem. Some storage is fine, but too much storage is a mistake.

The temptation for you right now is to continue to use your storage spaces to mask your "stuff problem." Out of sight, out of mind, right? It seems so much easier to put off till "someday" the hard work you know it will be to sort through everything you've got stored. So let's go make a sandwich.

Not so fast.

The tougher—but smarter—choice is to choose now to drastically reduce the number of things you're packing away and then to change your approach toward storing unnecessary items so you don't ever get such a buildup in your storage spaces again. Remember, our goal was the entire house. Yes, there are a lot of items in those spaces and therefore the thought of removing a big percentage of them can be daunting, but you brought them into the home and you can take them out again. This is doable. Trust me.

Back in 2008, I had done a good job of going through the basement in our Vermont home—I thought. But three years later, when we moved into a smaller home in Arizona with no basement, I was shocked at how much stuff we could still get rid of. Now I understood what we had been doing: rather than making the decisions to part with items one at a time when they became unnecessary, we had just stashed too many in the basement, leaving the reckoning for another day. In preparation for moving, I eventually got through all

---

SHOULD WE FEED THE LANDFILL?

If it's not possible to sell, donate, or recycle something, the only option left for minimizing our unwanted objects is to put them in the trash— that is, start them on their journey to the landfill. When we have a lot of objects to get rid of at once, such as when going through a crowded storage room, we might even have to rent a dumpster to make the removal efficient. And all of this makes a lot of people hesitate.

I get it. Who wants to contribute more to the buildup of the world's "trash mountains" than necessary?

My advice is this: use the other methods of eliminating items from your home as much as you can, but at the same time don't let your laudable sensitivity for the environment stand in the way of doing the most thorough minimalism home makeover you're capable of.

the excess storage, and I was glad I did. But before I was done, I started calling our basement The Ultimate Just-Because-I-Have-the-Space Area.

Do you have a space like that? The day of reckoning has come!

What I want you to keep in mind as you're sorting through your storage is that you're doing something good for yourself. Whether we're talking about stuff that resurrects harmful memories or just stuff that you know you should have gotten rid of a long time ago, you'll be glad you're taking action to minimize the burden from your home and life. You'll be alleviating the drag the past has on you through all that stuff, and consequently you will be able to more nimbly enter into the future.

If there's a new season of life coming up for you, such as retirement, now's a good time to clear the way for it.

If you're anticipating a move, you'll be more ready to go. (You don't want to move three hundred thousand things, do you?)

The undeniable fact is that every object in your home already exists. The resources have already been pulled out of the earth and manufactured into something. If you can't recycle it, presumably it's never going to become usable raw materials again. It just is.

So then the question becomes, *Where* is it going to exist? It is already taking up space somewhere on planet Earth, namely inside your home. If you send it to the landfill, it will be taking up an equal amount of space in a location that the authorities in your area have designated for disposal and are managing in a way designed to protect the public well-being.

Let your regret about how much you have to throw away reinforce your determination not to buy so much in the future. Don't let it inhibit you from making your home a silent argument for consumer restraint.

If you're anticipating an addition to your family, now's the time to be clearing space for the little fella.

If you're planning to downsize to a smaller home, this is an essential step to take in preparation for the move.

If you are worried that your loved ones will have a bear of a job sorting through your stuff after you're gone, you can act now to make it easier for them.

Of course, even if you don't anticipate a move or major life change of any kind, you'll enjoy the open spaces and efficiency when you've purged your storage and can easily find what you need.

Let's get right to the steps for minimizing your Ultimate Just-Because-I-Have-the-Space Area, wherever in your home it may be. Afterward, I'll help you reconsider your attitudes toward some specialized storage areas you may have: a hobby/craft area and a toy room.

★ STEP-BY-STEP MINIMIZING FOR YOUR STORAGE AREAS

Expect minimizing your storage spaces to take time. These spaces are filled with items that took years or decades to accumulate, so it will take more than one day to get through it all. For me, it was a multiweek process to minimize our basement in my spare time. Set a realistic schedule for yourself. Perhaps it would help for you to break the area into smaller segments, finishing one shelf, one corner, or one wall at a time. Being persistent and methodical will deliver the win. Because you've followed the easy-to-hard method, you've built up good momentum and your decluttering muscle is ready for this challenge.

By the way, although I often think that trying to sell the items we don't want anymore can be more trouble than it is worth, that may not be so true in your storage areas. Here you may find some things, such as an antique desk or old silver, that you can turn into real cash. So be on the lookout for a payday opportunity.

1. Remove Unnecessary Large Items

When I set out to minimize our basement, the first thing I did was to enlist the help of a strong friend to remove a piano that had been left there by the previous owner. Instant space! Similarly, you'll make quick gains and give yourself room to maneuver in the storage area, if you look for large items you can remove at once.

A piece of furniture that you could never find a good spot for in the home. A broken floor lamp. An artificial Christmas tree that looks too shabby to display in December. An exercise bike you rode every day for about a month, a decade ago. You don't even need to think much about whether to get rid of this kind of stuff. *Boom!* Gone.

Open space, just like that.

2. Get Rid of Smaller, Nonsentimental Items You Don't Need, a.k.a. Junk

After eliminating big stuff, target smaller items that have no important memory attached to them and have also lost whatever utilitarian value they may once have had. This, too, is easy stuff to minimize. I remember getting rid of tools we weren't using, an old dartboard, empty cardboard boxes, and a lot more. What can you toss from your storage area with little hesitation? Tear into it.

3. Get Rid of Collections of Stuff from Previous Seasons of Life, a.k.a. Junk in Bulk

As we go along in our lives, we tend to collect stuff that is important to us in each season of life. But a funny thing often happens—in a later season those things don't mean nearly so much to us anymore. Now we can get rid of them with hardly a pang.

In your storage space, you may have boxes full of mementos from high school, papers and textbooks from college, souvenirs from a trip taken long ago, clothes your kids have outgrown, and much more of a similar sort. Go through these groups of items to see if any are still particularly meaningful to you. I suspect there are a lot of them you can take one last fond look at and then slide into the trash bin without regret.

While cleaning out our basement, we found a box of several hundred of our printed paper wedding napkins. To be honest, I'm not sure why we kept them in the first place. Believe it or not, over the years, we just hadn't found the right occasion to use light blue napkins that read "Joshua and Kim, June 12, 1999." So now we decided to use them during our family meals for a few weeks until they were gone. It was a fun opportunity to tell our kids about our wedding.

4. Reduce Holiday Decorations

Most of us pack away holiday decorations in our storage spaces. These collections have a way of growing over time, often due to after-holiday sales that seem like such a good deal at the time.

Pull out these decorations and group them by holiday, taking stock of what you've got. Keep only the ones that mean the most to you and work best in your home. Move the others out for good. If you're near a holiday season (Christmas, for example), you may find it helpful to put up all your related decorations and then minimize after the season when putting things away.

Choose a physical boundary (say, two plastic bins) as the maximum space you're going to allot to holiday decorations. The next time a holiday rolls around, if you collect new decorations, get rid of some older ones so that the total quantity remains the same. Remember, just like before, displaying only the most meaningful decorations brings greater significance to them.

5. Pare Down Your Sentimental Items to Only the Best

Most of us hang on to things we've inherited or received as gifts from others, or that we ourselves have put aside, because they have memories and emotions attached to them or they have historical significance. These aren't mere holdovers from the past. These are heirlooms, records, and keepsakes that have unique meaning and that we have a harder time parting with.

An old family Bible. Grandpa's pocket watch and military medals. Grandma's china and silver tea set. Letters your spouse sent you while you were courting. The christening gown each of your children wore in church. Sure, you're going to want to keep some of this kind of stuff—less is different from none. But you don't need to keep it all.

Your goal should be to keep only the best. For example, you don't have to

---

PET PARADISE

Did you know that over half of people around the world own at least one pet? Argentina, Mexico, and Brazil have the highest percentage of pet owners. In the United States, the most popular pets are dogs (50 percent), cats (39 percent), fish (11 percent), and birds (6 percent).[2]

Pets are great, but unfortunately our furry, finned, and feathered friends can become a cause for clutter in our homes. Americans spend more than $2 billion annually on pet supplies, such as litter boxes, crates, leashes, fish tanks, and pet toothpaste.[3] And of course cat tiaras and Christmas-themed dog sweaters.

How much of this stuff is really necessary? Some of it . . . but far from all. Wild animals manage in nature without store-bought stuff; domesticated animals can be happy in our homes with less stuff than we typically buy for them. In fact, a simpler approach to the supplies that we keep would actually make caring for pets easier.

If you have a pet in your home, remember that the happiness in animal ownership comes from the pet, not from having a bunch of nonessential pet products.

hold on to everything you inherited from your beloved aunt who has passed. Just keep a few pieces that remind you of her most, and then, instead of keeping them in a dusty box in your storage area, put them out where you can see them and remember her every day.

If this is still difficult for you, set a goal for yourself. Maybe you can at least halve this collection of emotion-soaked stuff. I think you will find that setting a physical limit helps you quickly separate the *most* important from the *just-kind-of* important.

One thing that might help is to take photographs of things you're going to get rid of. After all, the memory is in you, not in the object. A digital photograph can evoke the memory just as surely as a bulky item can.

Similarly, scan old letters, documents, and photographs, and then get rid of the originals. This way you can access the information whenever you want and share it easily with others.

Sometimes we think we're honoring our departed loved ones by keeping their stuff, but let's ask ourselves if they would want us to be burdened by their belongings. Doubtful. The best way to honor those who loved us is to live our best life possible, not to be weighed down by their things.

In the same way, we do not do ourselves favors when we cling to past seasons of life after we have entered into new ones. You may have loved mothering young kids, for example, and look back on those days with great fondness. But if your kids have grown and have families of their own, you are in a new stage of life and should embrace it fully. Holding on to a lot of mementos of motherhood and longing for those days may be hindering you from fully entering into the potential of your new time of life.

For the Love of It

It can be a beautiful thing when people engage in hobbies or arts and crafts. It means they understand that life is not all about earning and spending money. We each have personal gifts to develop and an individuality to express. Active experiences make our lives richer, and our creativity makes the world lovelier, in ways that really matter.

Are you into fishing? Gardening? Sewing? Bicycling? Wind surfing? Skiing? Mechanical tinkering? Golfing?

Do you like painting watercolors? Knitting? Scrapbooking? Photography? Woodworking? Sculpting?

Whatever it is, good for you for being so active! But these kinds of pursuits do tend to accumulate stuff, don't they? Serious overnight backpacking, for example, requires a backpack, hiking boots, trekking poles, maps, a compass, a first-aid kit, a water filter, specialized food, specialized dishes and utensils, a stove with fuel, a sleeping bag, and a tent.

Think less about who you were. Focus more on who you are becoming. #minimalisthome

---

Where do you keep your hobby or craft materials? Maybe you have a room dedicated to this purpose, or at least a part of a room. You've probably also got a cabinet or closet where you store your supplies so that you can pull them out when you've got some free time to do what you love.

How do you minimize these things?

First, make a distinction between (1) hobbies or arts and crafts that you actually do; and (2) those that you used to do, or thought that you would do, but don't really do these days. Let's take a look at the second case first.

If you've got supplies for a hobby or craft that you don't pursue, then I can understand why it might be emotionally hard for you to get rid of the stuff. You might regret having given up that pursuit. You might wish you'd had more talent or perseverance in that area. But if there's no realistic chance that you'll get back into this pursuit, then the choice is actually easy—you should say goodbye to the stuff. Grieve a little if you need to. Learn something about yourself if you can. But at the same time that getting rid of these reminders of a former or failed avocation will declutter your house, it will most likely also help you move on from the past and be ready for new and more rewarding pursuits in the future.

Francine Jay says minimizing can cause us to recognize and get rid of our "fantasy self"—an identity that we tried to create by buying stuff that never really fit us. "We're empowered to evict that fantasy self and all her accouterments," Francine said. "It may seem cruel and heartless and difficult at first, but I promise you this—you'll feel a huge sense of relief when she's gone."[4]

Now, for those artistic pursuits or hobbies you are still actively engaged in, pull out all your supplies, look at them, and ask yourself if you can simplify the collection. How could less be more here?

Maybe it would be more relaxing and enjoyable to quilt if you didn't have so many fabric scraps, spools of thread, cutting mats, rulers, clips, and scissors on hand. Keep your favorites and hold on to the most useful items, then eliminate the rest. Neatly organize what you decide to keep. Maybe you'll end up removing some things that were unintentionally blocking a beautiful window view. Your craft room is going to become a place you love going to even more.

Whatever your hobby or leisure-time pursuit is, spend more time doing your thing and less time handling your stuff.

Even if one of your goals in minimizing is so you'll have more time and money for your favorite hobby or passion, don't go overboard with it. Think before you buy. Rely on that bias you've cultivated toward getting rid of things instead of holding on to them. Is there a benefit to owning less stuff related to your favorite free-time activity? The answer is probably yes.

The Deferred Camping Trip

Scott and Lisa Tower live in Mesa, Arizona. Well, when Scott isn't out driving, he lives in Mesa. Scott is a long-haul trucker, and he's on the road three hundred days each year. Lisa has been a stay-at-home mom for the last twenty-four years.

Their children have entered into early adulthood, and life change is in the air. As one season of life comes to an end, a new one begins to emerge—but not without some regret.

Scott, you see, has always been in love with camping. Lisa as well. Over the

---

FREEDOM

I was stunned to see a picture of a friend of mine standing in front of the charred ruins of his home, which had burned in one of the California wildfires. It wasn't the extent of the damage that was stunning to me, although there was nothing left of the home but blackened rubble. What stunned me was the smile on my friend's face.

He later explained that smile to me. He said that, first of all, he was relieved that his family members were all safe. But also he was feeling a kind of buoyancy about all the possessions that had been lost. He knew he would miss some of them, but he was pleasantly surprised by how unconcerned he really was about most of them. He was even sort of happy not to be responsible for them anymore.

Most of our stuff we could get along just fine without if we had to. Even the sorts of things we often put in storage—collections, keepsakes, and mementos—aren't terribly important when weighed against relationships and intangibles such as faith, hope, and love. We don't need a catastrophe to prove this to us. We can give ourselves that same freedom by eliminating the excess from our homes—all the way to the back wall of our storage space. And then we can use that freedom to cultivate things that really are worth giving our lives to.

Smile.

years, they have collected shelves and shelves of camping gear—tents, tools, stoves, hammocks, and so on.

"I had dreams of taking our kids on regular camping trips, sharing precious time and my love of the outdoors with them," Scott told me. "But I never took the time off work to do it. 'Maybe next year,' unfortunately, became my mantra—three words I now regret ever uttering in the first place."

Four years ago, Scott and Lisa were introduced to the idea of minimalism while attending one of my speaking events at a church in Scottsdale. With fervor, energy, and passion, they sought to minimize their home. Eventually, they stood face to face with the shelves and shelves of camping gear Scott had collected over the years. At their ages, sleeping on the ground in a tent had lost its appeal. They knew the gear had to go.

But the camping supplies weren't like other things they had already removed from their home. "To me, those supplies represented something that never was," Scott said. "It represented all the times I didn't take off work to spend a weekend outdoors with my family. The older they got, the more difficult it was to orchestrate schedules. Eventually, 'maybe next year' ran out of years.

"It killed me inside every time I looked at the camping gear. It was full of memories I thought I would have had. But now I never will."

While packing up the supplies, Scott whispered to himself, "What am I going to do with all this stuff?"

But then it hit him. His middle son, Logan, then twenty-two years old, was recently married. Despite not having gone on a family camping trip for almost fifteen years, Logan had a love for the outdoors that seemed to know no bounds. "He loves being outside even more than his father and I do," Lisa mentioned. "His wife too."

It didn't take long for Scott and Lisa to know exactly where their unused camping gear needed to go. They would gift it to Logan.

But not without an important conversation.

"As I dropped off the camping gear at my son's place," Scott said, "I took the opportunity to have a heart-to-heart conversation with him about living intentionally, spending time with family, and making the most of every day. I hope he'll take his wife and his kids camping someday, many days, and build wonderful, lifelong memories with them.

"'Use these supplies,' I told him. 'Don't let them just take up space on a shelf.'"

The seasons of our lives may change, but our opportunity to fully embrace and enjoy the current one has not. Make sure your home reflects your current opportunities.

Child's Play

Some folks have a separate playroom or toy room for their kids to play in, apart from the family room or the kids' bedrooms. A toy room for kids is a lot like a hobby space for adults, if you think about it. Isn't playing every kid's hobby? And a toy room collects a lot of items, some still being used and others languishing in neglect. A toy room is another place where things arrive and often overstay their welcome.

Wanting to free up space in the toy room actually isn't the most urgent reason for reducing the number of your children's toys. How about this for a motive? It's been proved that having too many toys actually reduces the quality of children's play. A study showed that toddlers with fewer toys focused better and played more creatively.[5]

If your home has a toy room that's overstocked, you'll want to work with your kids on this minimizing project. But first, you have to get them to agree in principle that removing some toys, games, and gaming devices from their play area is a good idea. Be careful with this because you may appear to your children to be striking at the very heart of their self-interest! (Interesting, isn't it, how early our clinginess with possessions begins?) Here are some lines you might want to use to make your case:

- "Do you ever have trouble finding a toy you want? That will be easier when you have fewer of them and keep them better organized."
- "Some of your toys and games take up a lot of space when you're playing with them. Making room in your play area will give you that space."
- "Remember how you tripped on that toy and hurt yourself? That kind of thing is less likely to happen if you don't have so much stuff cluttering up the room."
- "Don't you get tired of picking up toys when Mommy and Daddy tell you to? Now you won't have so many to pick up!"

When you've got your minimalist munchkins on your side, start with the easy grabs. Get rid of duplicates, toys your kids have aged out of or lost interest in, and anything that's broken, missing pieces, or too dirty to clean. There are probably a lot of items that fit these categories.

After eliminating the obvious targets, take stock of the total number of toys and games that are left. If it still seems like too many to you, and it probably does, talk with your kids about getting rid of some items even though they may still like them. With so many toys left, you can eliminate some and the kids will probably never miss them. (Complaints of "I'm bored" and "There's nothing to do" don't mean that our kids don't have enough to play with; they mean that they're still learning how to make good use of their time.) Target large toys to open up maximum space. If you can convince your kids to give up sets that have lots of small pieces, you'll reduce clutter fast. Eliminating noisy toys will reduce the "sound clutter" in your home. (You're welcome.)

With kids' toys and games that are still in good condition, you may have some donation possibilities. Give them to your church's preschool? A homeless shelter? An orphanage? A school? A children's hospital? Make sure you've got your kids with you when you're dropping off the toys at the donation site. There are more than a few donation center volunteers who will notice those little faces next to you and take the opportunity to praise them for what they did in giving up their toys for a good cause—a life lesson in fifteen seconds.

When you've reached your agreed-upon minimum, set a confined physical space for what you've got left, whether this means bins, shelves, or cabinets. Once the space is full, there is no room to add more toys. Help your children understand that principle by clearly marking the boundaries. If they want to add (think holidays and birthdays), they'll need to remove first. This is a helpful exercise for kids. After all, kids who don't learn boundaries become adults who don't set them.

Minimize your kids' playtime possessions and you may find that they become less selfish and less materialistic, cherish more and take better care of the toys they do have, and have more time for reading, writing, art, and imaginative play. They might spend more time with real live human beings. They might even go outdoors!

The Therapeutic Uses of Minimalism

Minimizing forces us to confront our stuff, and our stuff forces us to confront ourselves. That can be true all over the house, but it's particularly true when we get to the kinds of things we typically find in our storage, hobby, and play areas.

Expect this stage of minimizing to stir up emotions and recall memories both sweet and bittersweet. You may encounter old photo albums whose pages you haven't turned in decades, mementos of celebrations long gone by, trophies you formerly sweated to win, personal objects you remember being in the possession of loved ones you've lost, the wedding dress you wore before you had an inkling that you'd get divorced, the stuffed bunny your daughter fell asleep clutching throughout infancy, and art supplies you once envisioned yourself creating beauty with. The experience at times may warm your heart and at times may fill you with sensations of regret, loss, or failure.

Don't back away from the emotions. Work your way *through* them. This might be just the opportunity you need to process the past and position yourself better for the future.

Does the memory associated with an object cause you to smile? Your reaction may show you that you need the object, not for utilitarian purposes, but for purposes of the heart. But then again it may not. Maybe all you need is this one last moment to savor the nostalgic charm that the object inspires. Your life has moved on—maybe it's time for the object to do the same. Remember, just because something made you happy in the past doesn't mean you have to keep it forever. Decide rationally whether you should keep the object or whether the memory alone is enough to hold on to.

> Be remembered for the life you lived—not the things you bought. #minimalisthome

Does an object uncover buried feelings of pain? What does this tell you about how you've dealt internally with what happened in the past and what you might still need to do about it? Maybe you need to embrace the season of life you're in and let go of the ones that are past. Perhaps getting rid of an object or collection of objects would be a cathartic act, the beginning of a new stage of healing for you.

Who knew that "mere" decluttering would cut so deeply to the heart of us? Or that minimizing would cause us to journey inward to such an extent?

Minimizing Checklist

How will you know when you've cleared out enough clutter and excess from your storage, hobby, and play areas? Ask yourself these questions:

In the storage room . . .

☐ Do the sentimental items I have kept encourage me to look
   forward in life with confidence and optimism?

☐ If I were to die today, would caring for this room and its contents be a burden to others? Or have I gotten it to a point that it would not be burdensome for them?

In the hobby room . . .

☐ Does this room's environment inspire me to partake in my hobby?

☐ Do the supplies I have kept inspire me in my hobby or distract me from it?

In the toy room . . .

☐ Does every toy have a clearly designated "home" that my children can understand and remember when picking up their toys?

☐ Do the number and types of toys in this room encourage quality play that will spur healthy development?

Your Second Chance to Make a First Impression

Decluttering the Garage and Yard

I was first introduced to minimalism in 2008, after spending most of a Saturday cleaning out my garage. I didn't wake up that morning thinking I'd spend the entire day sweating in the dirty, dusty garage, but that's what happened. One project led to another, which led to another. You know how it goes.

After hours of effort, I noticed my five-year-old son swinging alone on the swing set in the backyard. I took another look at the pile of possessions in my driveway—all the stuff I'd spent my entire day taking care of. And suddenly I had this realization: *Not only is everything I own not making me happy, but even worse, it's distracting me from the things that do bring me happiness and purpose and fulfillment in life.*

My journey to minimalism, intentionality, and life change began in the garage, and rarely a day goes by without my considering the significance of it.

Your garage is where we'll *finish* your minimalism home makeover.

For practical reasons, I've saved the garage and yard for last because they often contain so much diverse and difficult stuff to deal with—everything from overflow storage from the house, to greasy tools, to lawn care products, to children's outdoor play gear, to much more. In retrospect, it's not surprising to me that it was my frustration with cleaning my garage that finally led me to break the grip that consumerism and materialism held on my life.

Minimizing your garage and yard is likely going to be hard work for you. But at the same time it is going to be rewarding because the yard is on display for you (along with everyone else in the neighborhood as well as your guests) to see, and the garage is probably the first place you encounter when you come home.

What do you want your first impression of your home to be every day when you return? You don't have to face clutter and mess, as you probably do now. Instead, you can experience spaciousness and order. What's even better is that it's going to be not just a practical reality but also a metaphor for

---

Inspiration

TAKING CONTROL

A community yard sale and neighborhood bulk-trash pickup was set for a weekend in July. It was the perfect opportunity for my wife and me to not just sell some of the things we had removed from our home but also finally tackle the overfilled garage.

As we began combing through boxes in our garage, we opened up one filled with wedding gifts in Bubble Wrap. Neither of us could even recall during which move we had wrapped them. We had simply moved that box—and countless others—each time we relocated to a new home. At that point, we knew we had to finish the job and fully minimize the contents of our garage.

When everything was finished, our garage looked cleaner than the day we moved in. Literally. The previous owners had left more than one corner full of things in the garage when we moved in.

It's a completely different feeling when I return from work now. There are practical benefits: finding things quickly, being able to walk

the new life you are creating for yourself—a life of openness, freedom, and opportunity.

A Home for More Than Just Cars

When Henry Ford and other early carmakers sold the world on automobile travel, they also set the stage for the appearance of the garage. At first people repurposed their carriage houses or barns for storing their automobiles, but soon most car owners wanted spaces specifically designed for their vehicles and preferably attached to their houses (apparently they smelled better than horses). By 1925, real estate agents were already finding it harder to sell homes without

around the car without squeezing against boxes, and feeling less anxiety about the garage that I knew needed to be cleaned.

But the benefits go beyond that. My minimized garage helps me feel more in control of my life.

I never noticed it before, but returning from work after a crazy day and pulling into a cluttered garage reminded me of the uncompleted projects at home. It was like a constant nagging feeling in the back of my mind that there were too many things to juggle in my life. My possessions were not only taking up physical space in my garage; they were also occupying mental space in my mind.

My garage now is filled with only things that bring value into my life. It feels intentional, like I am in control, not that my things are in control of me.

Because my garage has been minimized and the clutter has been removed, now when I get home, my mind is able to focus immediately on the most important things in my house—my family.

—Dallin, USA

garages.[1] Forty years later, "the average American garage accounted for an incredible 45 percent of the square footage of the entire home."[2]

As the rest of the home has grown, the garage no longer represents such a large part of it. Still, most of us apparently can't live without one. By 2014, 79 percent of homes in the United States had a garage or carport.[3] And whereas at one time most garages were large enough to accommodate just one car, today the two-car garage is by far the most common size for new homes in America.[4] Three-car, four-car, and even larger garages are becoming more common.

> You might get 85 years on this planet—don't spend 65 paying off a lifestyle you can't afford.
> —Cait Flanders #minimalisthome

Our garages are growing even as the average number of cars per household has been gradually declining over the last decade.[5] Could that discrepancy be because we're using our garages to help accommodate our overaccumulation of stuff? In fact, many of us have so much stuff stored in our garages that one car stays in the driveway or at the curb—a constant reminder of our garage-crowding problem. And for approximately a quarter of Americans, "the garage is so unorganized it can't even fit one car."[6]

A cluttered garage isn't doing a good job of serving its purpose of housing our automobiles and the products they need. Also, a cramped garage is difficult to maneuver our way through. Many of us are adept at the Garage Shimmy, a dance step whereby we squeeze out of our car door and then sidestep the stuff in our garage to get to the entrance to our home. If we're skilled enough at this balletic wiggling, we *might* keep our clothes from getting smudged by brushing against the side of a dirty car.

Using the garage for storage isn't wrong, but we can go too far with it. What have you got in your garage? If your garage is typical, I think I can predict some of the categories of stuff you're storing there.

First, there's car-related stuff. Cars have gotten so complicated in recent years that fewer people tinker with their own automobiles than in the past, so there's less need to keep automotive tools around. But still, we may keep some car stuff around, such as a jack to raise the car or fluids for topping up.

If you use your garage as a workshop, you've got a substantial additional set of things for projects around the house, such as a workbench, sawhorses, safety gear, work gloves, and a toolbox full of things like measuring tools, hammers, drills, screwdrivers, wrenches, cutting tools, and electrical testers. Then there are the inevitable cans or boxes full of grimy spare parts—nuts, washers, bolts, nails, and the like—that you didn't want to throw out because you thought you might use them one day.

A lot of us also use our garages to store lawn and garden supplies. Some of these, although probably useful, are quite space consuming: lawn mower, rakes, shovels, trimmers and edgers, chain saws, axes, and snowblowers (unless you live in Phoenix!). Others may be smaller but numerous: trowels, pruners, gloves, watering cans, spray attachments, potting soil, fertilizer, insecticide, and weed killer.

DRIVEWAY CLUTTER

They say the two best days for owning a boat are the day you buy it and the day you sell it. The same goes for a lot of our other large, expensive outdoor vehicles.

Got an RV or camper? An ATV or four-wheeler? A speedboat, bass boat, or canoe? A dirt bike? A snowmobile?

Let me ask you, Is it worth it to you?

You may get a lot of value from recreational "toys" that you keep in your driveway or elsewhere on your property. But if you don't, then their considerable expense and troublesome upkeep make these obvious items to minimize, probably by selling them. These kinds of "toys" are often easy to rent or borrow for occasional use, saving you lots of money and hassle.

Most of us also keep fun-time stuff in the garage: bicycles, skis, snowshoes, scooters, skateboards, in-line skates, wagons, sleds, lawn games, balls, badminton sets, hockey sticks and nets, gear for camping or hunting or fishing, golf bags, kites, sidewalk chalk.

And then there's the miscellaneous because-we-don't-want-it-in-the-house category comprised of such things as leftover paint, a ladder, garden hoses, ice scrapers, extension cords, carpet remnants, and spare floor tiles.

It's a lot. But it's not too much for you to handle!

★ STEP-BY-STEP MINIMIZING FOR YOUR GARAGE

Want to fit in a car that hasn't been under the roof of your garage for years? Curious about what's in those dusty boxes on the high shelf? Wish you could encourage the kids to go outside to play more often by making it easier for them to grab their yard toys? Eager to forget the Garage Shimmy and be able to walk comfortably into your house at the end of the day? Declutter your garage.

1. Remove the Products of Your Own Minimizing

At an event where I was speaking in my hometown of Phoenix, I talked to one woman who was in the process of minimizing her house. She had already decluttered most of it, and she was loving the change.

Then I asked her how it was going in her garage.

She averted her eyes briefly before admitting it was a problem, not so much because of the stuff she and her husband had been storing in the garage all along, but because that was where she had been putting piles of stuff she'd removed from the rest of her house! So much so that she couldn't even park her car inside it anymore.

Now, I understand that when you're removing things from your home, you might need a place—possibly your garage—to temporarily store them. But if that's what you've been doing with your garage, its use as a way station must come to an end. Your excess is not gone until it has left your property (not just your house). Transfer your unnecessary stuff to your trash or recycling can for removal or put it in your trunk to take to a donation center.

2. Get Rid of Trash

I'm not necessarily talking about literal trash here; most garages have a lot of things that just need to be thrown away.

I had a collection of leftover wood from a swing-set project in one corner of our garage, along with a whole bunch of other things that just needed to be thrown away—old golf balls, toys that had been broken or outgrown, a stack of manuals we didn't need, tools that had been replaced but not discarded, and even filters for a car I no longer owned.

How about your garage? Work your way through the shelves. Take a peek in storage boxes and bins. Get rid of all your obvious candidates for decluttering—those odds and ends and leftovers and orphans you've got sitting in the garage. If you can get rid of large items, so much the better because you'll give yourself more room to work.

3. Reduce the Amount of Kids' Playthings and Sporting Equipment

Most families have kid stuff in the garage, and these collections may no longer match what the kids are actually using.

For the transportation modes, pay attention to what your kids are taking out to play with. I know kids can go through phases, but if your son hasn't used his skateboard in two years, maybe he's outgrown it. I also don't see any need to have more than one type of item (such as one bike and one scooter) per kid.

For toys and sports supplies, I urge the same philosophy in the garage as in the bedroom and toy room—set physical boundaries and allow your kids to manage them how they want. In our garage, we have a shelving unit in the corner and one plastic bin. The plastic bin is where my kids can keep the balls they play with outside. The shelves are where they store their outdoor toys. As things collect and begin to overflow, we ask them to make decisions about what to keep and what to get rid of.

4. Dispose of Hazardous Items Safely

If you can get rid of motor oil or other hazardous chemicals or flammable materials from your garage, that's great. Just make sure you're doing so in accordance with the laws and guidelines in your area. For example, you can dry out brake fluid in a pan of kitty litter. Possibly an automotive shop with a coolant recycling machine would accept your leftover radiator coolant.[7]

ALTERNATIVES TO OWNING

Did you know that the average electric drill is generally used no more than thirteen minutes in its lifetime?[8] Yet how many of us have drills in our garages?

One of the reasons our homes become so cluttered in the first place is that, before we buy stuff, we buy in to the assumption that we should be stockpiling everything in our homes that we might ever need. Even if we haven't used something in years, we hold on to it "just in case."

The truth is, we don't *all* have to own *everything*. We could just own the basics and the things that are personal to us and then find different ways to get hold of more rarely needed goods and services as we need them.

The following alternatives will help you save space and reduce clutter in many areas of the home, but they are especially useful in the garage and yard.

---

5. Minimize Tools Until You Have Just the Ones You Need

I've never been an especially handy fellow, so I've always wanted just the bare minimum of tools—quality ones. I keep the most essential (screwdriver, hammer, tape measure, razor blade, a few others) in an easy-to-access space. The others (saw, some hardware, window squeegee, level, electric drill) are in one medium-sized box in my garage, not left out in the open.

If you are a DIYer, have a wood carving hobby, or use tools for your work (handyman, farmer, mechanic, painter), you're certainly going to have a different requirement for owning tools than someone like me. Nevertheless, be smart about your tool collection because there could still come a point where having too many tools becomes a burden. When you're ready to launch a project, do

- *Borrowing.* If you just keep the basic tools in your workshop, you might occasionally find yourself in need of an unusual tool for a specialized project. If so, don't go out and buy it. Ask a friend or acquaintance to let you borrow his.

- *Renting.* Sure, you *could* own your own pressure washer, but the reality is that years are going to go by between times when you pressure-wash the exterior of your home. Rent a pressure washer as needed instead. If the rental fee for this or another tool seems steep, remember that you're saving the purchase cost as well as the "clutter cost" that comes with storing any item you own.

- *Hiring.* If keeping the lawn mowed and the shrubbery trimmed isn't something you enjoy, then maybe you could get rid of *all* your lawn care equipment and hire a lawn care company (or neighbor kid) to do that work for you. According to one study, "People who spent money to buy themselves time, such as by outsourcing disliked tasks, reported greater overall life satisfaction."[9]

you want to waste your valuable time digging through a pile of unused tools to find the one you want?

6. Pare Down Your Outdoor Hobby Gear

A lot of outdoor hobby stuff, such as camping, fishing, and rock climbing gear, collects in the garage. If you have these kinds of collections, think carefully about which items you actually need and which ones you don't. Remove outdated, broken, or already replaced items, along with any items you simply never use.

You might be able to remove an entire hobby collection if it's been years since you took part in it or it represents a different stage of life. Get rid of the old hobby clutter to make room for new passions.

Today is the day to rid yourself of anything that distracts from your best life. #minimalisthome

---

By paring down your outdoor hobby collections, not only will you be making your garage more spacious but you might also be making your outdoor hobby more fun. For example, you might have your best time ever on your next fly-fishing excursion if you can easily pack up to go and therefore can focus more on fooling trout.

7. Organize What's Left

Don't stop minimizing before your garage looks spacious and manageable. And when you're down to what you really need to keep in your garage, organize neatly what's left so that it stays clean and you can find it. I recommend the use of containers in this area of the home. Maybe you could organize your brooms and shovels with tool hangers. Place things on shelves to get them up off the floor. Fill plastic bins and label them.

Your garage is now ready for you to drive into at the end of the day, and it's ready to launch a new project whenever you are.

Curb Appeal

Now let's step outside and enjoy the fresh air for a moment. There's one more place to minimize: the yard.

Not everyone has, needs, or wants a yard. But if you've got one, then you know that it, just like your house, can contribute to the feelings of clutter, mess, and distraction you feel. On the other hand, if you minimize it well, you can turn it into a space that creates the context for a peaceful, orderly, and lovely place to live.

Minimalist Home Value

NATURAL LIVING

If I had any doubts about whether minimalism is a good thing (which I haven't in a long time and never will again), all I would have to do would be to remind myself of how perfectly minimalism interlocks with other great human ideals.

Ideals such as peace, restoration, cleanliness, health, beauty, and order.

Responsibility, restraint, focus, and a concern for others and our common home, the earth.

Intentionality, individuality, humility, restraint, frugality, and in-difference to society's everlasting hustle.

Contentment, gratitude, and generosity, along with creativity, growth, productivity, and optimism.

And do you know what part of the minimalist home reminds me of this constellation of magnificent values the most? It's the yard, or as our Brit friends term it, the garden. The home's setting (if we will just desist from cluttering it up) offers a peaceful meeting place for people and nature.

About 60 percent of people in the United States live in detached family dwellings and therefore have a yard to take care of.[10] It may be postage-stamp size, or it may be a substantial acreage, but it's usually a valuable and versatile space. The front yard often presents a more public face, while the backyard is typically more dedicated to family fun. If you can pry them away from their electronic devices and shoo them out the door, your kids will learn to love playing in the yard and will create many memories there. Gardeners dream about springtime and creating living beauty in their yards. Yards provide space for pets to roam. A yard can be a wonderful place to invite friends over to enjoy a picnic and watch the sun set. Even the driveway can be a place for shooting hoops or trying out a new pair of skates. Again, we can see specific purposes for this.

Despite all these advantages of owning a yard and the traditional importance of a yard to family life, the size of yards is actually decreasing these days. The average lot of a new home in the United States is now 0.19 acres, down 13 percent since 1978. The reason for the shrinkage, apparently, is economic: today's bigger houses cost more, and one way to save money is to buy a smaller lot. One journalist commented, "Forced to choose between having a bigger lawn and a bigger house, Americans who live near economic hubs are picking the house."[11] The same phenomenon is occurring in Australia and other nations.[12]

Minimalism can't make your yard bigger, but it can help you make the most of the yard you've got. Maybe, through minimizing, you'll get out more, enjoy nature more, have more outdoor fun with your family, get more exercise, and interact more with your neighbors. You know—exactly what a yard is for!

★ STEP-BY-STEP MINIMIZING FOR YOUR YARD

What are your goals for your yard? To create a place of peace? To grow beautiful things? To have an outdoor space the kids and their friends will want to play in? To spend less time taking care of it? Minimalism can help with all of these goals.

1. Remove Decorative/Ornamental Items

Garden centers are happy to sell us yard decorations, just as home decor stores push decorations for inside our homes. Whether inside or outside, we don't need as many decorations as most of us have. If your yard displays a lot of decorations, especially kitschy stuff of the garden-gnome or plastic-flamingo sort, rethink the wisdom of that. Please. (I speak on behalf of your neighbors here.)

Maybe you don't need any yard decorations at all—the landscape's beauty may stand out all the better without any artificial adornment. If you do want yard decorations, don't use too many of them, and keep them simple and tasteful. Some kinds of yard ornaments and accessories, such as water features and birdbaths, can help to create a natural environment that conveys peace and charm.

Carry the less-is-more approach over to outdoor seasonal decorations as well. Using a smaller number of well-chosen Christmas or other holiday decorations can be just as festive and a lot more elegant than a bunch of glittery, whirling, blow-up, lighted, and musical decorations. A simple set of holiday decorations will also require less time for setup and takedown and will occupy less storage space in the off-season.

2. Eliminate Unnecessary Outdoor Furniture

Does your yard have furniture in it? A patio set beside a grill, perhaps? Or a picnic bench? How about a hammock strung between trees? Seats encircling a fire pit?

Can you thin out the furniture? To help you make the decisions, think about which pieces help you enjoy the outdoors and which pieces mostly just clutter it up.

3. Remove Unused Play Items

Homes with kids in residence tend to have a lot of play items in the yard—rope swings, play sets with slides, trampolines, swimming pool, sandbox, tree house.

I know you want your kids to have fun in the yard. My wife and I like to have a fun yard so that our kids invite their friends to our house and we can keep an eye on things. Still, it's possible to overdo it.

What outdoor play items are your kids no longer playing with? Take them away.

Are there any that are broken or that stand out as contributing to the cluttery look of the yard, perhaps because they are so large? Remove these.

Teach kids to put outdoor toys such as soccer balls and badminton rackets away where they belong after the kids are done playing with them.

4. Simplify Your Gardening

People like me who love gardening understand how relaxing and rewarding it can be to work in the soil to create a beautiful flower bed or a vegetable and herb garden. The patience and cyclical nature of gardening are a lovely match for the ethos of minimalism, standing against the hurry and greed of an acquisitive society. So if you garden in your yard, good for you! Give yourself more time to spend enjoying your plants by minimizing your gardening gear. It's just like cooking or indoor hobbies: you can do more with less.

Keep the gardening tools you find yourself going back to over and over. Get rid of the ones that just sit on the shelf. Favor standard tools over gimmicky gadgets. Gardening isn't a fancy hobby, and you don't need to get fancy with your gear.

Anything else you can get rid of? Pots and trays you brought home from the plant nursery and don't need anymore? Duplicate watering cans you could reduce to one? A bent trowel or that set of support stakes you never use? Simplify.

And enjoy.

May the bouquet of flowers you gather from your garden stand out like a work of art in your minimized homescape.

I hope the fresh herbs and vegetables you harvest in the backyard will inspire you to create delicious, fresh dishes in your clutter-free kitchen.

5. Transition to a More Natural, Easy-to-Care-For Landscape

A living environment is always changing. That's part of the fun and the challenge of having a yard. It's also an opportunity. You can make changes in your lawn, trees, and shrubs so that your yard will be simpler to take care of and create the experience you want. This isn't instant minimalism, but it *is* minimalism you can start as soon as you're ready.

Could you reduce the area of grass that you have to mow, replacing the turf with hardscape such as gravel?

Use water-thrifty perennials instead of thirsty annuals?

Replace imported species with native ones that are hardier and require less watering and work on your part?

Your landscape is the ongoing work of art inside the frame that is your yard.

You Did It!

To your neighbors and people who drive by, your minimized yard will be a statement about the priority of natural beauty and peace over clutter. When you tap the garage door opener and drive into your minimized garage, a sense of peace will surround you even before you get out of your car. We've gone not only from easier to harder but also from inside to outside, and now your home is ready to welcome you into its domain of calm and order.

The garage/yard area of minimizing is the capstone of the transformation you've given to your house. Review it all. As you stroll from one uncluttered room to another, what spacious areas delight you the most? I'm sure you're going to love your "new" home, where you can dwell in comfort while being better able to focus on people rather than on things and to live a more intentional life.

The Minimalist Home is not done yet. I still have to show you how to keep your home minimized. Also, I've got some very important things to say about ways you can capitalize on your hard work of decluttering. But for now, savor your achievement and celebrate it with your loved ones.

Your home minimalism makeover is complete. Good for you!

Minimizing Checklist

How will you know when you've cleared out enough clutter and excess from your garage and yard? Ask yourself these questions:

For the garage . . .

☐ Is this garage a welcome sight when I return home each day?

☐ Does my garage communicate calm and control?

☐ As much as possible, is it easy to maneuver in my garage?

☐ Am I no longer embarrassed to leave my garage door open and allow the neighbors to see inside?

☐ Am I confident I have removed everything from my garage that is no longer needed?

For the yard . . .

☐ If applicable, does my outside space bring me joy when I look at it or spend time in it?

☐ Does the outside of my home communicate hospitality?

Action recommendation: *To mark the completion of your home decluttering, have a friend over to share lemonade on your porch and hear your story. Or invite some neighbors over for a barbecue and show them around the place while the burgers are grilling. Bask in the beauty of your home and newfound freedom.*

Minimalism Maintenance Guide

Becoming minimalist is one thing. Staying minimalist is another.

If you've followed the step-by-step guidelines of the preceding chapters, you've decluttered your entire home. It may have taken days, weeks, or months. But regardless, it was a one-time process. You're done with that.

I hope—and believe—that you're loving the results. I bet you feel like you can "breathe" and relax in your home in a way you haven't in a long time. I imagine you're excited about devoting more of your time, money, and energy to the people and the passion projects you care about.

Don't you want to keep those good feelings going?

You can. It's a matter of instituting routines to keep your home clutter-free. Fail to follow these routines, and I'm afraid you'll find yourself living in the same cluttered home you just spent so much time and effort minimizing. But keep them going, and you'll find that you're still enjoying the benefits of minimalism a month, a year, even ten years from now.

For this purpose, I'm going to give you some guidelines to follow daily, weekly, periodically throughout the year, and in different seasons of life. Some of these guidelines might seem onerous at first glance, but trust me—after you've minimized your house, they really aren't a hardship. Maintaining your minimalism, in fact, is a whole lot less work than having to repeat your minimizing if you let your home get cluttered again.

In a way, it's ironic that I'm writing a book about living uncluttered. For much of my life, I left beds unmade, failed to put books back on the shelf, filled the sink with dirty dishes, and dropped clothes on the floor. But minimalism changed the nature of the chores in our home, and it changed me too. I live differently now in the kitchen, the bedroom—all over the house. I changed. So can you.

To avoid any misunderstanding, let me point out that this minimalism maintenance guide isn't about cleaning. It's not about wiping the baseboards or dusting your fine furniture. It's also not about repairs and what we usually refer to as *maintenance* around a home—things such as fixing a broken window latch or replacing the furnace filter. As necessary as cleaning and repairs are, what I'm referring to here is keeping a home minimized, efficient, and effective for the people inside it.

HOW TO CHANGE YOUR BUYING HABITS

Overbuying was the biggest reason you got in your clutter mess in the first place, right? Now that your home is minimized, you have to buy less if you're going to stay minimalist.

It's always better to avoid bringing home a new item that you don't need than it is to have to get rid of it later. Apply the *Do I really need this?* question before an item crosses over from being in the retailer's possession to being in yours. Here's help:

- *Avoid triggers.* Ask yourself why you have overbought in the past. Does boredom inspire you to go recreational shopping? Does buying something make you feel better about yourself for a little while? Do you engage in impulse shopping to show off in front of your friends? Find a better way to respond when these emotional triggers activate.

- *Impose a temporary shopping moratorium on yourself.* If you think going cold turkey might help you break your addiction to shopping, pick a period of time (maybe ninety days?) when you'll buy nothing but consumables, such as

Since every home and family are different, some of the following guidelines may not apply to you, and there may be others you could think of to add to the lists for your home. But start with these lists to establish regular home-care practices that keep your home easy to live in and easy to love. Thumb back to this section as often as you need to until these routines become like second nature to you.

Now, will you always be perfect at keeping up with these guidelines? Of course not! So don't feel burdened by this advice. Just be as regular with these routines as you can, and that should be enough.

---

groceries. Just live with the clothes, books, tools, and other durable goods you've already got. You'll probably find it's not a hardship at all and will help you break a bad shopping pattern.

- *Become a savvy buyer.* By this, I mean understanding the strategies that marketers use to convince you to buy things you don't need. Don't be seduced by sales tactics or let yourself feel pressured by limited-time offers. Calculate in your head the "clutter cost" and add it to the price tag. Is the benefit greater than the burden or the other way around? You're the buyer, so you should be in charge of the shopping experience and buy just what you intend to.
- *Be calculating about your shopping.* Do product research and make purchases online when appropriate. When going to brick-and-mortar stores, consolidate your shopping to the minimum number of trips. Make a list and stick to it. When you get home with just what you need and no more, congratulate yourself and think about the money and hassles you saved yourself.

DAILY Maintenance Guidelines

Clutter attracts clutter. If you drop the mail on the kitchen counter, someone else is going to find it natural to leave his keys there. A dresser with receipts is also going to collect coins. A purse dropped in the entry is soon going to be

RESTORING GIFT-GIVING SANITY

According to the National Retail Federation, the average shopper in America spends almost $1,000 on gifts during the winter holiday (mainly Christmas) season.[1] In addition, most of us receive several presents for our birthdays. And then there are all the other gift-giving occasions throughout the year, including Valentine's Day, Easter, and Mother's and Father's Days. And don't forget special occasions, including wedding anniversaries, baby showers, housewarming, graduation, recovery from sickness or surgery, thank-yous, baptism or confirmation, bar mitzvahs, and "just because." That's a lot of stuff coming into our minimalist homes from well-meaning friends and family!

Gift giving can be a beautiful thing. But if you're determined to avoid returning to overaccumulation in your home, then you're going to have to manage the gift-giving traffic in your home.

- *Tell your friends you don't need a gift.* If you let them know you'd rather have well wishes in person, or maybe a greeting card, that's better than getting yet another decorative candle or bottle of bath salts you don't need. Change the gift-giving expectation.
- *Request quality over quantity.* If requesting no gifts is going to be a tough sell with some people in your life, encourage them to purchase quality over quantity. This is especially helpful when

joined by shoes and gloves. An empty soda can on the end table usually winds up with a few candy wrappers next to it.

When you're diligently tidying an area daily (which isn't hard if you stay on it), you are less likely to lose control of that area. If you see any space in your home that gets cluttered with unnecessary things more frequently than every

---

influencing gifts given to your children. Two $25 gifts are usually less clutter than ten $5 gifts.

- *Ask for consumables instead of durables and experiences instead of material goods.* A fruit basket, a gift certificate to a restaurant, movie passes, a bouquet of hand-gathered wildflowers, show tickets—these are great gifts that don't burden your home with new possessions.

- *Suggest donations to charities on your behalf.* It feels great to know that the money that could have gone toward a new sweater you don't need instead went to a school scholarship that changed the life of a child.

- *Let people know what you need.* Even after minimizing, you may have some genuine need for new items in your home, such as a coffee maker to replace the one that died last week. Let people know ahead of time what your real needs are; be specific. Gift lists can be particularly helpful for out-of-town family members, especially when ever-growing and changing kids are involved.

- *Purge guilt-free.* As the value of the gifts you receive begins to reveal itself, eliminate the unwanted ones without feeling guilty about it. You've expressed your appreciation—you're not obligated to hold on to the object forever. Nobody wants to burden you with a gift.

two or three days, it's a place that you should put on your daily habit list. These
practices will get you started:

Straighten up the bedroom. Make the bed, put away clothes, and
   unclutter dresser tops. Establish rules with your kids about
   straightening up their own rooms.

Put paper where it belongs. Stay on top of incoming paper and
   office clutter by handling it the day it arrives. Junk mail and
   newspapers in recycling. Important papers in folders.

Put back toys. Realistically, life doesn't allow a clean toy room every
   evening. But if you have a toy room apart from your family
   room, spend sixty seconds returning toys to the places where
   they belong. Or better yet, get your kids into the practice of
   doing it themselves.

Clean up homework. Teach your kids the habit of putting away
   their schoolwork each night before bed rather than scrambling
   around in the morning trying to find it.

Tidy the living room and family room. High-use areas can be
   cluttered and disarranged by the whole family. Walk through
   at the end of each day and straighten up these spaces.

Store media out of sight. Put away all video games, charging
   cords, and computer accessories that were used during
   the day.

Check the entryway. Particularly if the yard is snowy or muddy, you
   may need to organize the boots, coats, and other things in your
   foyer or mudroom. The cooler the weather, the more layers get
   shed just inside the door.

Reset the kitchen. Wash dirty dishes and put them away. Likewise, put away utensils or pots and pans that don't belong on
   the counters. It's a wonderful thing to go to bed knowing that
   you'll wake up to a clean kitchen for breakfast.

Return things left out in the bathroom. When we're in a hurry getting ready in the morning, it's easy to leave out things such as hairbrushes, makeup applicators, razors, and blow-dryers. Rectify that problem when you get home by putting everything back where it belongs.

WEEKLY Maintenance Guidelines

Stuff regularly enters our homes. It comes in from school, church, the grocery store, shopping, online stores, gifts, and so on. But most of us don't have regular routines to remove these items, so they just seem to stay with us. These weekly cleaning tasks provide opportunities to reverse the flow:

Take out the trash and recycling. Use this time not just to toss garbage but to look for things around the home that you can remove.

Wash, dry, fold, and put away the laundry. As you're doing this, notice wardrobe items that never or rarely show up in the laundry, because if they're not getting worn, that's a clue you can probably get rid of them.

Clean the bathrooms. Any empty product containers or other items you can get rid of? The larger your family, the quicker the containers of consumables are going to empty.

YEARLY Maintenance Guidelines

Different seasons, turning points, and special occasions that we cycle through each year offer opportunities for refreshing the minimalism of our home. Make creative use of these times to bring your home minimalism up to date:

After Christmas and birthdays. If you or your kids received toys or other presents, are there any that you want to regift while they're

still new? What old things can you get rid of to make room for
the new ones you're keeping?

After any holiday you decorate for. Is it time to retire any of the
holiday decorations? Take down and neatly put away the ones
you're going to keep.

After filing your taxes. What papers can be digitized, shredded, or
recycled?

Spring cleaning. Embrace the old tradition of using springtime to
do a deep cleaning and purge of unneeded possessions in your
home.

The annual neighborhood garage sale. A garage sale is a time-
consuming way to make very little money. But maybe your
neighbors don't know that and you can add your items to the
sale they are having in their garage.

The start of a new school year. Reevaluate your kids' clothes,
backpacks, and school supplies. What new things do they need,
and what comparable amount of things can you get rid of, so
that you can maintain the equilibrium?

**The transition from the warm season to the cool season, or vice
versa.** If you have different sets of winter clothes and summer
clothes, take a look at what you've got when the time comes to
switch. Maybe some items have been outgrown or just never
worn. As you're looking at them afresh, you may see some you
just don't want anymore.

LIFE SEASON Maintenance Guidelines

We all go through major life transitions, though they aren't necessarily the
same ones and may not come at the same time or in the same order for all of
us. With each transition, the *Do I need this?* question becomes relevant in a

new way because of our new life context. We may need to reminimalize ourselves each time—and we'll find new benefits from minimalism that help us
make the most of our current season of life.

**Are you finished with your college studies and starting your
career?** Getting a full-timer's paycheck can be intoxicating, and
consumerism's temptations will be strong. Now is the time to
develop the habits of thinking carefully before buying anything,
determining to choose quality objects that will last, and taking
good care of your possessions.

Are you getting married? Be strategic and restrained about what
you put on your gift registry. And know that you're likely to
have a lot of duplicates you can get rid of when you merge your
spouse's stuff with your own. Work with your husband or wife
on developing a shared philosophy of minimalism—this
partnership will make living minimalist easier for the rest of
your life.

Are you adding a child to your family? Don't give in to the false
I-need-it-all mentality about parenting gear. Make a list and be
rational in your purchases and gift requests. Set up a simple
nursery or kid room that enables you to spend more time with
your child and less time taking care of his things. This is a
chance to start minimalist parenting practices you'll build on for
years to come.

Are your children going through their own transitions? From
babies, to toddlers, to preschoolers, to grade-schoolers, to early,
mid, and late teens, our kids go through changes faster than we
do. Of course they'll need new clothes and toys as they grow, but
with each round of shopping you can exercise restraint in what
you buy as well as purge items from the previous stage of your
children's lives. As they grow, revisit and reinforce boundaries

with them, helping them to gradually take more responsibility for maintaining minimalism in the home as they mature.

Are you getting a new job, enduring a period of unemployment, trying out a different career path, or starting a business? Maybe you can get rid of some old tools or work clothes to offset the new ones you're bringing in. Maybe you should rethink what you need in your home office. Maybe you can sell some of your stuff to give yourself more ready cash.

Are the kids starting their adult lives outside your home? Or have you lost a spouse through death or divorce? When loved ones leave your home, of course you will grieve the loss. But when the time is right, look at their stuff that's left in the home, keep a few of the best as mementos, and get rid of what you can.

Is someone moving back in? It seems like it's more and more common these days for an early-adult child to move home while establishing a career or for an elderly parent who needs assistance to move in with a son or daughter. If you have a boomerang child coming into your home, explain your minimalist beliefs and put some boundaries on what she can bring with her.

Are you retiring? Can you remove the clothes you wore to your office when you were working? Is it time to rethink your leisure-time possessions? How can you simplify the workload around the house to make things easier for yourself? Make the most of your retirement by spending less time on your home and more time on activities that keep you healthy and happy. Your best legacy isn't going to be the possessions you pass down; it's going to be the good you do, the relationships you build, and the memories you leave with others.

PART 3

Future

A Small Suggestion

If you choose to downsize to a smaller
home, you'll be able to multiply the benefits
you've already acquired through minimizing.

A couple of years after we minimized our home in Vermont, my blog was getting to be known and I was starting to get interview requests with journalists. One humid morning in August 2010 I was sitting on the back porch of a relative's home in Nebraska while I answered questions over the phone for CBS's Christina Hernandez.[1]

At one point she asked me about any "sticking points" as I tried to practice minimalism.

As good interview questions often do, this one pressed me to reflect on my personal experience of minimalism. After a bit of thought, I told Christina that my two big remaining minimalism goals were to get rid of one of our two cars and to downsize to a smaller home.

Not long after that, my wife and I experimented with using only one car . . . but soon went back to using two. I still think the goal of having just one car—or even *no* cars—per family is a great one for many people to have. But for us, in a busy season of life with two kids and two jobs, and living in an area with limited public transportation, keeping two cars seems wisest.

We were more successful with my other goal of downsizing to a smaller home when we moved from Vermont to Arizona in 2011.

The housing market was considerably cheaper in the Phoenix area than in our Vermont hometown, and we could easily have embraced a massive upgrade when we moved. That's what many people in our situation would have done. That's what *we* would have done before we discovered minimalism and its benefits. But as it happened, we never even considered buying a larger home. Instead, we looked forward to moving into a smaller one.

Actually, the smallness of the home wasn't even particularly a goal of ours in itself. We were looking for the optimal home for us—one that fit our young family and promoted our values. It was just that, as minimalists, we knew that an optimal house would be a relatively small one.

Less house, more home. Downsize.
#minimalisthome

I was moving to Phoenix to work at a church, and we wanted to live in the same neighborhood where the church met, so that answered the location question for us. As for the house itself, our final list of nonnegotiables consisted of three bedrooms, a dining room and family room sufficient for entertaining, pleasant outdoor surroundings, and high-quality craftsmanship in the home.

We were thankful to find a house that fit our criteria exactly, with no unnecessary extras. Its benefits were great and its burdens were minor. In moving, we reduced our home size from over 2,200 square feet to less than 1,600 square feet. At the same time, we cut our mortgage payment nearly in half, while enjoying higher quality construction, and found that we could spend even less time and money in maintenance than for our home back in Vermont.

Because of our experience and my observation of others who have benefited from downsizing, I'd like to make a small suggestion to you (if you'll excuse the pun): might the next step for you be moving into a *smaller* minimalist home?

I realize downsizing is not for everyone. Possibly you already live in as small a home as your family could get by with. Maybe you love your newly minimized home so much now that you wouldn't dream of leaving it. Those are great reasons for staying put.

On the other hand, after what you've done in minimizing your home, maybe you've already begun to see downsizing as the logical next advance to make. Maybe you've realized that you don't really need both a living room

DOWNSIZING FOR THE DECADES

The advantages of downsizing when you're younger

So many young couples buy the biggest house they can afford as soon as a loan officer says they can be approved for it. And thus they start out a lifetime of carrying heavy mortgage debt. What they don't think about is the flexibility and freedom they're giving up in exchange for square footage.

If yours is a younger family, buy only as much house as you need and don't strain your borrowing capacity more than you have to. Lay the groundwork of a lifetime where you—not lenders—are in control of your financial well-being and lifestyle.

The advantages of downsizing when you're older

As people get into middle age and beyond, if they've accumulated some savings and some equity in their home, the assumption is often that they'll "reward" themselves with a bigger house. And yet, if their nest is emptying out at about the same time, they may have less need than ever for a big house.

If you are reaching a point where you have more financial resources, stop to think about the kind of house that would really serve your desired lifestyle best. It might be more about location, configuration, or construction quality than about size.

and a family room. Maybe the closets and storage spaces that used to seem inadequate now seem excessive. Maybe the guest room you thought was going to get used never is. Maybe you just realize now that your home has more square footage than your family needs. And as a consequence, maybe it's time to minimize not just the possessions inside your home but the home itself!

On average, an individual will move eleven times during his lifetime.[2] Eleven percent of US citizens move every year.[3] So you may have an occasion coming up soon when you'll need to think about the kind of new home you want anyway. Moving into a smaller home could be a timely transition for you to start planning. Now might be the time to start applying the *Do I need this?* question to your entire home.

Whether or not you've been considering downsizing to this point, let me encourage you to read this chapter. I'll be focusing on the benefits of owning a smaller home—and there are a lot of them. For sure, moving is a chore, even after having minimized your possessions. Nevertheless, if you can pull it off, downsizing is an opportunity for you to make huge additional gains in living simply and intentionally.

Moving into a smaller place isn't confining. It opens up so many new possibilities!

Reasons and Seasons for Downsizing

There's hardly a more obvious statement that one is choosing to move against the culture's bias toward more and bigger everything than deliberately moving into a smaller home.

House sizes have been steadily increasing for decades. In the United States, the average new home size in 1975 was 1,645 square feet.[4] In 2015, just forty years later, the average new home size was up to 2,687 square feet.[5]

At the same time, the average number of persons per household has been dropping slightly—from 2.94 in 1975 to 2.54 in 2015.[6] So the amount of living space per person, on average, has been increasing even faster than the size of our homes. The same trend is happening in most developed nations around the world as affluence expands and fertility rates decline.

For many people, a large home is seen as an obvious positive: Why wouldn't you live in a large home if you can get one? Certainly it's anyone's right to think that way. And if someone has a large family, I would agree that a home with several bedrooms might be what that person needs. Nevertheless, I know—and by now *you* know—that with bigger homes comes a greater drain on family finances, more space to fill with possessions, and more work to maintain it all.

I'm thankful that it appears many in our society are starting to question whether moving into bigger and bigger homes should continue to be a goal for us. A survey conducted by real estate website Trulia shows that, of those home-owners currently living in homes larger than two thousand square feet, a clear majority—60 percent—would choose a smaller home if they were to move.[7]

1975
Average home size: 1,645 square feet
Average household size: 2.94 people

2015
Average home size: 2,687 square feet
Average household size: 2.54 people

LIVING SPACE AROUND THE WORLD

Average residential floor space per person (in square feet) in selected countries:[8]

Australia: 960	Japan: 379
United States: 832	United Kingdom: 356
Canada: 779	Spain: 373
Denmark: 702	Italy: 335
Germany: 587	Russia: 237
Greece: 484	China: 215
France: 464	Hong Kong: 161
Sweden: 425	

Are you among the majority who are thinking small instead of thinking big about their next home? Maybe the time is coming up soon when you'll want to sell the place you've got and move into another home that's cozier, with everything closer at hand and requiring less maintenance. Downsizing could be a great way to position yourself better for the future you've got in mind.

Retirement is still the life passage that causes most people to choose to move into a smaller home. But there are actually a lot of appropriate seasons of life when you might choose to downsize. For example . . .

- Your last "baby" has gone off to college.
- You've gotten a divorce or suffered the loss of a spouse.
- You've taken a new job and it requires you to move to a new area.
- Your income has dropped, making the mortgage and maintenance expenses tougher to cover.
- You're having health problems and it's getting harder to keep up with things around the home.

And there's one more:

- You've turned into a mighty minimalist, and you just want the advantages that come with living in a smaller home!

Whatever your motivation for downsizing, you're going to love the benefits that come with this change. Let me highlight a few:

1. *More money.* We'll be getting into this advantage in more detail shortly, including the exceptions to the rule, but in general a smaller home costs less to buy or rent and less to maintain.

2. *Less time and energy spent cleaning and maintaining.* If you dislike these tasks as much as I do, you'll be glad to know that minimizing combined with downsizing will reduce the time you spend on these chores to the least amount possible.

3. *Better family bonding.* Some people think that having a bigger home, with lots of play and conversation areas, will be good for their family relationships. But my experience says the opposite: having more interior space tends to isolate family members in separate parts of the home. A smaller home naturally brings family members into proximity, leading to their having more conversations and doing more things together.

4. *Less environmental impact.* Today's home builders are using construction techniques that are more energy efficient than those of the past, but did you know that the growth in square footage of new homes has wiped out "nearly all the efficiency gains"?[9] If you move into a smaller home, however, you will be doing something good for the environment by using less energy and fewer natural resources.

5. *Easier perpetuation of your minimalism.* When you move into a smaller home, you'll pare down your belongings even more than you already have. Plus, you won't be as tempted to buy new stuff that you don't need—because there won't be room

for it anyway. It's easy to stay on the minimalism wagon when you're living in a small home.

6. *Wider market to sell.* Since a smaller home is also usually less expensive, when you eventually sell your downsized home, the price point should make it affordable to a large percentage of the home-seeking population. Therefore, you should be able to get out of your downsized home more quickly.

And those are just the general advantages to downsizing. Who knows what advantages you might find in a smaller home, even beyond what you were initially hoping for, after you move in?

Maybe you'll be inspired to become a more creative person when you take up residence in a quaint older neighborhood and get out of that suburban tract where you can have a house of any color as long as it's beige.

Maybe by putting your preadolescent kids in a bedroom together, they'll socialize better and develop closer bonds.

Maybe you and your spouse will rediscover each other when you're actually spending time together instead of tag-teaming on chores.

When the right time comes to move, the upside of downsizing is huge, including many personal and unanticipated benefits. That's what many downsizers have found, including Kay Emery of Omaha, Nebraska. I'm quite familiar with her story because she's my mother-in-law.

No Regrets

A few years ago, following the death of her husband, Kay moved from a 2,400-square-foot house into a much smaller single-floor condo. Nobody had to talk her into it. She was ready.

"After living in my house for thirty-three years, raising three kids, and caring for my husband through his extended fight with cancer," Kay said, "I was ready for a change. There were some physical characteristics of the home that were getting difficult for me as I got older, like walking up stairs. But more significant than that, I wanted a new start, a clean slate, a home that was crafted the way I wanted it to be for my next stage in life."

She admitted that the process of minimizing her possessions in order to move was not easy at first. There were lots of memories tied up in the thirty-plus years' worth of things in her home. She had to sort items from her children's childhoods, her recently passed husband's belongings, and sentimental items left by both her and his parents.

"My daughters came over and helped. It was hard at first, but eventually it became a freeing exercise for me. I was looking forward to a smaller home, but it was definitely difficult to see a dumpster delivered on the first day and face the exercise to come. But it didn't take long for me to get into the swing of it. I ended up hosting two garage sales, taking numerous trips to Goodwill, and filling an entire dumpster of things to remove—all within a short period of time. I couldn't believe it."

Whenever my family goes to visit Kay in her condo, she tells me she couldn't be happier in her new space. "I spend so much less time cleaning and so much less money on my home," she said. "Additionally, moving from a large corner lot, where I was responsible for all the shoveling, mowing, and upkeep, to a smaller lot maintained by the local HOA freed up my life considerably—both financially and in time and energy investment. I am able to go out and do things and be with my friends. I am able to travel with little notice. And I have less worry all around.

"Also, Joshua," she continued, "I am thankful that I have freed up my life to be present and supportive in my friends' lives when they need me. When my husband was sick, especially near the end, I needed my friends and they were there for me. Now I am able to be that person for others. At our stage of life, many of us are experiencing loss—loss of spouses and loved ones, failing health and physical abilities. I truly believe this downsized home has allowed me to be a better friend to those I love in the times they need it most.

"If I have any regret, it's that we didn't make the move sooner, when my husband was healthier and we could have enjoyed the freedom together. I've become a vocal advocate for downsizing, convincing several of my friends to do the same. Not a single one of them regrets it. We're having too much fun."

Downsizing by the Numbers

As I said earlier, when we downsized, it cut our mortgage payment in half. My mother-in-law saved money too. And I can tell you that probably you will see financial advantages when you downsize as well. But every home transaction is different, and it's not a simple equation. We have to look at the variables.

The reason that calculating relative housing costs when we move is so important is that housing expenses make up such a big part of the typical family's budget. For homeowners, housing expenses accounted for a little over 33 percent of the average US consumer's total expenditures during 2014.[10] And renters aren't doing much better. Sadly, "the median rent nationwide now takes up 30.2 percent of the median American's income, the highest cost burden" for rent since tracking began in 1979.[11]

Owning a home is just plain expensive. In November 2017, the average home price in the United States was $248,000.[12] The average mortgage loan is about $225,000, with a monthly mortgage payment of a little over a thousand dollars and total interest paid over the thirty-year life of the loan roughly equal to the principal.[13] And that doesn't even begin to count the upkeep. In 2016, US homeowners collectively spent $361 billion—an amount greater than the Gross Domestic Products of more than 80 percent of the nations on earth—on home improvements, maintenance, and repairs.[14] All those big houses we keep building are sucking up our hard-earned cash at an incredible rate.

Who is benefiting from all this spending? You? Or mortgage lenders, real estate agents, home improvement retailers, and others in housing-related industries?

Example: Savings from Downsizing	
Costs associated with a 2,467-square-foot home:	**Costs associated with a new 1,600-square-foot home:**
Purchase price: $303,441	Purchase price: $196,800
Down payment: $30,000	Down payment: $30,000
Monthly mortgage payment: $1,781	Monthly mortgage payment: $1,113
Monthly PMI (for 88 months): $228	Monthly PMI (for 38 months): $139
Monthly insurance: $145	Monthly insurance: $104
Monthly property tax: $291	Monthly property tax: $189
Monthly utility payments: $345	Monthly utility payments: $224
Average monthly costs for repairs and maintenance: $254	Average monthly costs for repairs and maintenance: $164
Total monthly expenses: $3,044	**Total monthly expenses: $1,933**
Total annual savings due to downsizing: $13,332 **Total savings over life of thirty-year loan: $378,448**	

Chart for comparison use only. Individual costs and savings may vary considerably.[15]

Why not try to keep more money in your own bank account? Your biggest expense is also your biggest opportunity to make a change in your financial situation.

The financial advantages that can come to you when you sell a large home and buy a smaller one may include the following:

- reducing or even eliminating your mortgage payment
- eliminating your mortgage premium insurance (if you're paying it now)
- lowering your property taxes
- lowering your property insurance

- reducing your utility costs
- reducing your maintenance costs

I say that these *may* be financial benefits, because it depends. For example, if you move to a higher-cost area, your new smaller home may be worth as much as your old larger home and therefore may have comparable mortgage payments, property taxes, and property insurance. Perhaps you'll even have new expenses when you move, such as condo or HOA fees. (But even in that case, a smaller home will result in more financial savings than a larger home in the same neighborhood.)

Utility payments and maintenance costs, on the other hand, are almost always less in a smaller home than a larger one, especially if you move into a well-constructed, efficient home.

"A major saving that comes with downsizing your home is the cost of utility bills," said Charlotte Local, director of conveyancing operations at Enact. "The fewer/smaller the rooms in a home, the less money you need to spend on heating them because the heat will be much better contained in a smaller space. Similarly, you will be saving money on electricity, having fewer rooms to light, also meaning you will have fewer electrical items to clutter up each room."[16] Downsizing from a three-thousand-square-foot home to one of just one thousand square feet "could reduce your monthly electric bill by as much as $200."[17]

At the same time our houses are getting bigger, our families are getting more broken. Coincidence? #minimalisthome

---

When we moved to the Phoenix area, one of the few things we didn't like about our new home was the carpets. If it had been a bigger home, we might have decided to just live with the disappointing carpets, since it would have been so expensive to replace them. But since this was a smaller home, we found the cost to get brand-new carpets would be quite reasonable. So we just went ahead and made the change to higher-quality carpeting—and loved the results.

Since then, we've found that many other upkeep costs, such as painting, floor cleaning, and even pesticide application, can be cheaper in a smaller home.

When you're calculating the financial effects of downsizing (especially when not otherwise required to move), you should also consider the one-time costs that come with any move:

- repairs or upgrades of your old house to make it more marketable
- travel expenses if you're shopping for a new home in a different area
- the storage unit you may use to temporarily store your stuff
- broker commissions
- closing costs
- moving expenses
- repairs or upgrades you want to make to the new house
- furniture or decorations you buy for the new place

These are going to add up to several thousand dollars. But if you're moving into a new home that's cheaper to live in, you should be able to make up these one-time costs within a year or over a few years at the most.

In the long term, and all things considered, downsizing means more money in the bank almost every time. Often a *lot* more.

So be thinking about what you're going to do with any financial windfall (profit from the sale of your old home plus any monthly cost savings you see) that comes your way after the move. Will you roll your home-sale profit into your new mortgage, thus cutting your monthly mortgage payment? Will you pay off credit card debt? Funnel money into investments for your retirement? Put your kids in a private school? Increase your financial donations to good causes? Travel? Start a new business?

Combined with the more personal, less tangible advantages of downsizing, the financial possibilities should be enough to make many of us start thinking about what it would look like to take the plunge and actually start looking for a smaller home to move into.

How to Buy a House That's Just Right for You

Think for a moment about how people normally go about buying a new house. Often, the first active step they take is to get preapproved for a loan. Then they look on the real estate listings and go out house hunting with a real estate agent, usually targeting homes at the top of the price range they can afford (sometimes even higher). While out shopping, they think, *Ooh, it would be nice to have a huge yard like those people have.* Or, *I love the high-end kitchen in that house.* Or, *I bet we'd totally use that movie theater setup in the basement.* In the end, their budget doesn't stretch as far as their house envy does, but they stretch it as far as they can and get as big and fancy a house as they can afford, already dreaming about the time when they can sell it and buy an even bigger one.

Buy the house you need, not the house you can afford. #minimalisthome

---

Having been through downsizing myself and talked to many others who have done the same thing, I now think there's a much better way to go about finding a house that's a minimalist's dream and not a materialist's fantasy. Like the Becker Method of minimizing, it's a culturally contrarian and highly intentional process. Consider this the Becker Method, Whole House Edition, for people who are ready to move to a smaller home.

When you're looking for a downsized home, start by asking yourself some questions. First of all, what *kind of home* do you want to have? If you are in a single-family dwelling, your new place might be a smaller single-family dwelling. But there are other options too. Do you want the low maintenance you can enjoy with a condo or apartment? Is it time to move into a retirement community? What about some of the more extreme or exotic options, such as living in an RV, tiny home, or container home?

Next, come up with a list of *must-haves* for your new home. Things like the part of town you want to live in, the type of floor plan that works for you, the number of bedrooms your family needs, the school district you want for your kids, and more. Write down a description of what you need. This is your guide.

Then, do you want to *rent or buy*? Both are valid options, and I'll soon be addressing the considerations for this decision in more depth.

If you have the time, money, and expertise, maybe you should consider the third option of *building* exactly the home you want on the lot you choose. In some areas of the country, this makes perfect financial sense, but you need to consider what you would be getting into with this option.

When you begin shopping for your new home to rent, buy, or build, *look for the smallest house* that fulfills those wants and needs. Don't even be a lookie-loo at big houses on the market, because they might inspire house greed. Don't let yourself be seduced by extras that you don't need and that would only require you to waste your resources to maintain.

Of course you should calculate *how much you can afford to pay,* both upfront (if you are going to buy or build) and on a monthly basis. But if you're thinking minimalist, this calculation is not a purchase-price target. It is a safety check to ensure that you don't overspend. The minimalist's home-buying motto is "Buy the house you need, not the house you can afford." Repeat it to yourself often.

Now *go house shopping.* Have fun doing it. Keep reminding yourself of all the benefits you're going to enjoy when you make the move. Buy when you find the small home of your dreams.

Smaller home, bigger life.

New Lease on Life

We own a home, like being homeowners, and think it makes financial and practical sense for our family to own a home at this time. But I have a feeling that, someday, our two kids are going to move out and leave us behind. Then it will be just Kim and me, and—who knows?—maybe then we'll sell our house and rent a place instead.

I once heard somebody (I wish I could remember who) say, "My dream is to rent an apartment in walking distance of a train station that can take me to an airport, where I can reach anywhere in the world." That's stuck with me. Maybe that's how Kim and I will live when we're older. You may pass us on a street in Kuala Lumpur or take a sightseeing boat ride with us in Rio's bay. We won't be worried about our apartment because it will be locked up safe and sound.

Inspiration

MORE WINGS THAN ROOTS

After Jeff and I got married, like most young couples with newly se-cure incomes, we assumed we should buy a home and "set down roots."[18]

And then Emma, the first of our three children, was born.

That's when Jeff and I began a conversation about how we really wanted to live our lives. We decided that we wanted a home with as little maintenance as possible, which for us meant no yard work, no shoveling, no home repair or renovations, and no mortgage.

We have many friends who are homeowners and enjoy garden-ing, yard work, and the pride of investing in their home. Sometimes I wish I found joy in those pursuits. But I don't. And neither does Jeff. And finally admitting that and taking the steps to move toward a dif-ferent life that is more authentic to who we are has been liberating.

The life we are building is focused on each other. On people. And experience. And while homeownership may be strongly tied to the way some families live out those priorities, for us it was a distraction from them.

My point is that there can be many reasons, at every stage of adulthood, for renting instead of owning a home. Supposedly, a part of the American Dream is homeownership. But do you know what? Who cares? If some other living arrangement besides homeownership enables you to live *your* dream, do that instead.

Weigh the benefits and burdens of homeownership, then do the same for renting, and see which option comes out on top.

The reason this is a downsizing issue is that rental units are typically smaller than houses available for sale. In fact, in contrast to expanding home

---

By renting, we have the freedom to let go of the what-ifs of the rest of our lives and embrace life as it happens.

Building a "forever home" requires predicting how many people will fill that home at any point. And how the space will be used from toddlerhood through adolescence.

Instead, we live in a space that fits our family and needs as they are now. And when those needs change, we have the freedom to move elsewhere with little hassle.

When the day comes that we're ready for long-term travel, we can plan without the stress of selling a house. And the investment account created by the down payment we didn't need can now be used for any number of investments that are more worthwhile.

Every day we walk out our door to a bustling block and wander across the street to a playground full of families. Or stroll to a beautifully groomed campus with almost limitless space for the girls to explore while I sit on a bench far away and enjoy watching their independence grow.

I'm at peace. This life fits us, and I'm so happy we chose it.

—Rachael, USA

sizes, apartment sizes in the United States have actually been shrinking. Between 2006 and 2016, the average size of a new apartment dropped by 8 percent to 934 square feet. That means the average US apartment is now about a third the size of the average new US home.[19] In the United Kingdom the average one-bedroom flat is even smaller—only 495 square feet.[20] Rising prices, urban crowding, and shrinking family sizes are often cited as reasons for today's small apartments.

There *are* large apartments and large houses for rent, of course, but if you're looking for a smaller place to live, rental units offer plenty of options. Still, you need to put size in perspective with other factors when making the buy-versus-rent call.

One other important factor is finances.

Over the long term, buying is generally a better financial option than renting. Unlike rental payments, which are subject to inflation and increase over time, a purchased home is a hedge against inflation. Your mortgage payment will remain your mortgage payment for the life of the loan, no change whatsoever. You can also deduct the mortgage costs from your taxes. Furthermore, home values generally go up over time, giving you more equity in the home.

In the short term, however, renting a home can be cheaper. Renting avoids the cost (and hassle) of buying and selling, which can take a while to make up with a growth in home equity. Also, because renting comes with one monthly payment that covers such things as trash removal and maintenance, this allows you to avoid extra and unexpected costs. If you're worried that a lack of home equity is going to put you in a financial bind later in life, you can put some of your financial savings from renting into investments.

But as important as the dollars-and-cents calculation is, what matters even more is that you're making the right choice to either buy or rent based upon your dreams and desires.

- Do you see yourself staying put and needing the same amount of space for a while? Do you like the feeling that your home fully belongs to you and you can do whatever you want with it? Does the gradual, steady accumulation of value in the home align with your larger financial goals? Maybe buying is better for you.

- Do you think you might want to move again soon? Do you want the hands-free lifestyle of a low-maintenance home? Are you worried that your income could become unstable? Would you enjoy the amenities of a rental complex? Do you want to travel for extended periods? If so, perhaps renting is the better option for you.

There's no right or wrong to the buying-versus-renting debate. All I'm saying is that if you are interested in downsizing, you should at least consider renting, based on a combination of practical and aspiration goals.

Sidestepping the Comparison Trap

I was at the house belonging to an acquaintance, Mick, one Friday afternoon. It was a larger-than-average house, with palm trees and a pool in the backyard. Although it was undeniably beautiful, it seemed a little excessive to me. Of course I didn't say anything about that because it wasn't really any of my business. I was there to get to know Mick better and talk over a project we were working on together.

While we were hanging out, Mick began lamenting the fact that he and his wife had friends coming over for dinner that night.

This seemed odd to me. I asked him, "Why would you not be looking forward to dinner with friends?"

He explained to me that, a few weeks earlier, he and his wife had been at a social function and had met a couple that they immediately hit it off with. Before the evening was over, they had all decided to get back together. In fact, they had decided to get together *twice* more—once for dinner at the other couple's house and once for dinner at Mick and his wife's place.

"So," Mick continued, "last weekend we went over to their house for dinner. Joshua, I'm telling you, it was the biggest house I've ever been inside. And everything was gorgeous—the furniture, the decorations, the meal.

"Now they're coming over to our house tonight, and I'm worried what they're going to think. It's not nearly as big as theirs."

I nodded and tried to look sympathetic, but in truth I was thinking to myself, *Wow, what a terrible way to live! To be constantly comparing yourself to what everyone else has. There is no joy in comparison.*

Yet this is how many people, not just Mick, live all the time. They buy the biggest, fanciest house they can swing, but there's always someone else who has a still bigger, fancier house. And the discontentment and dissatisfaction set in.

As a minimalist and downsizer, though, I can honestly say that I do not want to live in a bigger home than I have now. Ever.

When I drive through neighborhoods with huge houses, I say to myself, *Who changes the light bulbs in that thing? What a burden it would be to always have to take care of so much!* I know that the home we have offers just the right amount of space for me and my family. And since that's the case, I've lost all desire to live in a bigger home.

I've got to tell you—it's way better living life this way than it is to be constantly comparing and desiring something more than you have. As a matter of fact, I look forward to the day when people living in excessive square footage are more apt to be embarrassed by their homes than people living in just-right-sized homes.

When you're ready to downsize, get the house that's right for you, whether that's an efficiency apartment, a two-bedroom town house, a three-bedroom home for your family of five, or whatever it may be. The key is that it has what you need and no more. Don't ever be ashamed of it. Be proud that you've bucked the trend of society and sought out just the kind of home you need. And remember all the good things you have brought into your life and the lives of your loved ones by not wasting money on a house bigger than you need.

The people are the life of a home. Successful family living was never about the size of a house. So make more of the people within your household, and make less of the house itself.

This Changes Everything

Minimizing your home reveals new
possibilities and potential for your
life—so go after them!

It's been ten years since I decided to minimize my possessions. When I started, I had no idea of the changes it would bring about in my life. I just happened to hear the idea from a neighbor that maybe I should get rid of some of my stuff. That hit me at just the right moment, and—*bing!*—I was ready to declutter. In my naivety I didn't know what to expect. I came into minimalism with my eyes wide shut.

I started minimizing at home because of one goal: I wanted to spend more time with my family. I knew our excess stuff was interfering with that objective, and so I was prepared to clear out our clutter, whatever it took. Another way to put it is that more family time was the only mountaintop I was hiking toward at first. It wasn't until later that I saw another mountaintop beyond that one. And then a third mountaintop beyond the second. To my amazement, it turned out there were more and more things I could achieve by living with less.

I often say that minimalism has changed everything for me. And that's true. But I need to clarify what I mean by that.

My most deeply held values have not changed. My Christian faith was important to me before; it still is. I was devoted to my wife and kids then; the same goes today. I viewed my work as a way of making a positive difference in people's lives and my leisure time as a chance to enjoy the people I care about; nothing's different about any of that.

Faith, family, and friends—those priorities have remained unchanged for me. But with an uncluttered home and a new commitment to living a simple and free lifestyle, I have found more opportunity than I ever thought possible to pursue each of those priorities. And not just to pursue them but to actually accomplish things in those areas of my life in far greater measure than I had ever imagined before. Instead of just wishing or dreaming, I am doing!

Today I'm a better follower of Jesus because I understand how much my heart used to be tied to the things of this world and because now I am freed up to cultivate my relationship with him.

I'm a better husband because I have more time to spend on my wife and more resources to spend with her. And I'm a better father—more present in my kids' lives than I used to be and a worthier example for them.

The goal of minimalism is not just to own less stuff. The goal is to unburden our lives so we can accomplish more. #minimalisthome

---

My capability to speak helpfully into the lives of others has increased ten-thousand-fold—it's greater than I ever imagined it would be. This book is one example of that influence.

In all these areas and more, minimalism has changed me. It has created room for good things to emerge in my life. That's what it always does.

Now, at this point I should acknowledge what we all know to be true—that many people who are not minimalists accomplish great things. So it's definitely possible for materialists to do much if they are gifted and make a sufficient expense of effort. I just think it's *easier* for all of us to fulfill and expand our potential, and *more likely* for us to actually do so, if we waste less time, money, and energy in buying and caring for physical possessions we don't need.

As more and more of us minimize our homes, the cumulative potential for what we all can do to strengthen our character, build up our families, enrich culture, and meet needs easily busts through the limits of my comprehension. We, as a society, waste so much time and energy and money accumulating material possessions that we don't even realize how much good we could accomplish if we freed up those resources for better things. With our homes minimized, our lives are packed with potential to a far greater degree than we could ever predict. *Everyone's* lives. Even mine. Even yours.

When I told you way back at the beginning of our journey together that doing a minimalism makeover on your home would mean undergoing a makeover on *you,* this is what I meant. And it's going to change everything if you'll only choose to go where the journey takes you . . .

Crossing the Bridge from Dreaming to Doing

By this point, you have learned how to declutter every room in your home and have considered the possibility of downsizing to a smaller home. I hope you have also wrestled with bigger questions than simply how many towels to keep in your linen closet or what to do with the junk stored in the attic. I hope you have dreamed about what kind of family you want to have, how you will spend your newfound time and money, where you will pursue happiness if not in material possessions, and what kind of person you want to become.

As Gracia Burnham, who spent a year of her life as a prisoner of militant rebels, once said to me, "When everything is taken away, we begin to see who we truly are." Minimalism doesn't take away everything. But it does take away everything unnecessary. And it leaves us face to face with ourselves and the question of what we're going to do with the rest of our lives.

Minimalism doesn't change you all by itself. It creates a context where it's easier for *you* to change yourself. It offers you more abundant resources that you can use to try to accomplish whatever you want. Whereas being materialistic tied you up so much that probably at most you could only dream about doing many of the great things you wanted to, minimizing has built a bridge to actually doing those things. But it's up to you to take the steps and cross over.

As we've seen, your home has purposes, each room in the home has purposes, and the possessions in those rooms should serve those purposes. Most importantly, *you* have purposes too. Minimalism will help to reveal those purposes to you and make it easier for you to pursue them. Your part is to revisit and revise your goals, whenever needed, *and to act on them.*

As I defined it earlier, minimalism is intentionally promoting the things we most value by removing everything that distracts us from those things. That means creating a minimalist home is not an end in itself. Sure, having a declut-

WHAT DO YOU WANT TO BE THANKED FOR?

During a conversation we were having about how to make decisions, my friend Joe Darago said to me, "I just keep asking, *At the end of my life, what do I want to be thanked for?*"

I found his question to be profound and clarifying. If we ask it ourselves, it will cause us to define our life purposes, plan our legacy, and intentionally align our actions with our principles. It's not that we're greedy for recognition or affirmation; it's that we want to look at our behavior from the perspective of how it affects others. Even if we don't actually *receive* thanks, we've done the right thing if we *deserve* thanks.

As I've thought about it more, I've come to believe we can adapt my friend's question for different time periods and more specific contexts. For example . . .

- At the end of this workday, what do I want to deserve thanks for from my coworkers?

tered place to live is great. But beyond that, minimalism is a pathway to an end: a life of newly recovered passion, purpose, and margin in life to pursue the things that matter most. How good does that sound?

When you ask people what they most want to accomplish with their lives, nobody responds by saying, "I just want to own as much stuff as possible." Instead, we talk of love and faith and relationships and making a difference in this world. We talk of living a life of significance that positively influences the people we love the most. This—*this* is the purpose we are drawn to.

It's just that somewhere along the line, the world hijacks our passions and directs them toward things that don't matter. And slowly but surely we sacrifice a life of passion and purpose for those other things. But minimalism calls

---

- At the end of this week, what do I want to deserve thanks for from my spouse and kids?
- At the end of my year of volunteering on this service team, what do I want to deserve thanks for from the people we're helping?

These kinds of questions will influence your life daily, even hour by hour, if you let them. They will affect the words you use, the expression on your face, the attention you give, and the ways you choose to spend your valuable resources of time, money, and energy.

When I ask such questions, I almost always realize that I want to be thanked for being loving and attentive to my family, for being encouraging and a positive influence on others, and for living a life consistent with my words and my values.

What do *you* want to be thanked for? If you've minimized your home, giving yourself more room for reflection and intentionality, you can not only ask this question but also start living in a way that will enable you to earn the sort of gratitude you prize the most.

---

us back. It invites us to rediscover our potential—and aligns our resources to accomplish it.

Living a purposeful life is the most rewarding way to live. A science journalist investigating the connection between happiness and meaning concluded, "When we are deeply engaged in an activity that is in accordance with our best self, we often report the highest levels of life satisfaction."[1] Other researchers have shown that people who have a sense of purpose in life often live years longer than those who don't.[2] Even when a life of purpose is costly, the examples left by the greatest men and women in history show us that it can have enduring worth for the world.

So today, this very moment, where are you at in defining your purposes? And where are you at in pursuing them? Wherever you are, keep going.

Minimizing your home and not using its benefits to catalyze positive life change is like receiving a financial windfall and squandering it instead of investing it for the future. Cash in! Capitalize on the opportunities that minimizing your home has given you.

You broke the inertia that living with too much stuff exerted on you. You can break the inertia that merely dreaming of doing good things has too. The effort will be paid back many times over.

The Multiplier Effect

"Our journey into minimalism started because we needed to pay off debt," Dana Byers told me. "We began selling off lots of our things because we had to. It wasn't the best of circumstances, by any means."

She was talking about the time, twelve years earlier, when she and her husband, Chris, were going through the hardest struggle of their young married life. Their three-year-old son, Blake, had a life-threatening brain infection and required surgery. Dana had to quit her job to take care of him full time, and at the same time she and Chris had to figure out a way to pay off mounting medical bills.

Thankfully, Blake fully recovered. But the Byerses were never the same after selling their possessions.

Dana said, "The process forced me to revisit and reevaluate the path that I was on. It allowed us time and space to reevaluate our priorities in life. In more ways than one."

After minimizing, Chris and Dana felt called to adopt a Guatemalan girl with special needs. Adding Mackenzie to the family has been challenging at times, but now they can't imagine their lives without her. She is a beloved daughter and a full participant in their adventuring lifestyle.

Shortly after the adoption, Dana and Chris discovered a passion to serve others overseas. In order to pursue that passion, they sold off even more things—all they had, in fact.

Be remembered for the life you lived, not the things you bought. #minimalisthome

---

Dana described it. "At the age of twenty-seven, we held an estate sale and sold everything. People would walk up to the estate sale and ask us who died. We'd just smile. Nobody had died, except maybe our former selves."

Over the next two years, Dana and Chris would work in ten different countries, becoming pioneers in the online church movement. After returning to the States seven years ago, Chris started a successful data management company. Dana now serves on staff with a church in Indiana.

They can now afford to fill their home with all the furnishings and decorations, gadgets and goodies they want, but the thought has never seriously entered their minds. They live in an open, uncluttered home because they never want to lose that ready-for-anything mind-set they adopted when minimizing their old home.

I asked Dana to reflect on how minimalism has changed her. I'm going to quote her at length because she stated so beautifully the true riches we can find in life when we live with less.

Minimalism has helped me become more decisive and less stressed. Therefore, I am better able to pursue the legacy I always wanted but wasn't clear to me until I removed the unnecessary elements of life. It helped me break free to live my best life.

Once money is taken out of the conversation and you let values lead the way, you're going to find a way to bring it about. Once you break through that feeling of having to do whatever the world and society wants, you never want to go back.

I don't fear coming to the end of my days and wishing I'd found a way to multiply my efforts. Just the opposite—minimalism has been the multiplier effect on living my dreams and fulfilling a calling on my life.

Too often, we numb ourselves by covering up pain and sadness and frustration with buying something. But somewhere along the way, we also cover up passion and potential. Minimalism brings a sort of confidence. Like, who cares what other people think? And once you break through that barrier and get past the point of ever needing to go back, a whole new world of opportunity opens up for you.

★ STEP-BY-STEP MAXIMIZING FOR THE REST OF YOUR LIFE

I'm not a guru, counselor, or life coach. I'm not going to discuss mindfulness with you, delve into your childhood, or encourage you to map your future. And I don't want to make unwarranted assumptions about you, because I don't know exactly where your journey is taking you. Everybody is different.

But I have observed certain basic moves that I believe every new minimalist has to make at some time to reach out and seize the potential that having a minimalist home offers. These steps will get you well on your way across the bridge from dreaming to doing.

1. See the Potential in Yourself First

Minimalism is not about checking out on life. Just the opposite: it's about engaging life better. And that will never happen without a hopeful mind-set.

The way I look at it, somewhere between the hucksterism of "You can do anything you want!" and the defeatism of "Poor me, I'll never amount to anything" lies the truth. Positive thinking *is* powerful. It just isn't miracle working. But that needn't stop any of us from having a realistic faith that we can level up our significance.

So never, ever sell yourself short. With more resources in your kit thanks to minimizing your possessions, you *can* try new things and make changes that once seemed out of reach. So go ahead and dream big dreams about what you can do with your life. With your collection of stuff shrunk to a rational size, you really do now have the opportunity to expand in personal influence.

Back in chapter 2, my assurance about undertaking a home minimizing project was "You can do it!" I have the same assurance for you now about capitalizing on the gains minimizing has given you.

You. Can.

2. Allocate Your Resources to the Things That Matter Most to You

The second step in maximizing the rest of your life is to begin directing your resources toward those values you already hold dear—those things that motivated you to pursue minimalism in the first place. Maybe being debt-free is a high value for you. Great. Take the financial savings you're getting from minimizing your home and use it to pay down your credit card and loan balances. Or maybe traveling the world is important to you. Then plan your first trip itinerary, budget the money, set aside the time for it—and go!

Your highest values may never change in your lifetime. Or maybe they will. But regardless, start with what matters to you now and shift resources there. Along with these resources, you'll shift the emphasis of your life.

3. Learn When to Say No

In *The Minimalist Home*, we have focused on minimizing possessions around the house. But the skills we've acquired in weighing benefits against burdens with our household objects are skills we can apply in less tangible parts of our lives too, including our schedule, commitments, and relationships. We don't have total control over how we spend our time and who we spend it with, but we have some choices we can take back from others or from societal expectations. And saying no to distractions means saying yes to our dreams.

Just as some of our possessions are not bad but just not worthwhile enough to keep around, so some of the things we could spend our time on have some value but don't help us in achieving our greater purpose right now:

No, I can't work overtime this weekend. Little League season is coming up, and I promised my son I'd teach him batting.

No, I'd better not go to that cheesecake place after the movie. I'm halfway to my weight-loss goal, and I don't want to lose momentum now.

No, I won't be able to make it to the family reunion this year. I'm using up the rest of my vacation days to go with a team and help repair hurricane damage.

Thanks anyway, but I'm afraid not. (I've got something else great I've got to do!)

4. Nurture Gratitude; Grow Generosity

Minimizing your home gradually changes your attitudes toward both what you hold on to and what you give away. That is, it encourages gratitude and generosity. Both attitudes can help you in becoming the person you want to be.

- **Gratitude.** When you not only don't *have* too much stuff but also don't *want* too much stuff, you experience a contentment that the person who lusts after the latest gadgetry and crowds in more furniture will never know. When your collection of possessions is down to just the stuff you need, then you not only notice them more but also appreciate them more. You feel satisfaction and peace. Gratitude arises within, and that's a more attractive quality than greed will ever be.

Gratitude also reminds us that we have so much to give others—the connection to its twin attitude:

- **Generosity.** Minimalism allows you to live a more selfless lifestyle. If you're no longer trying to live a life of *get, get, get,* you can begin living a life of *give, give, give.* You become a generous person, the kind of person who waters this parched world of ours.

At first, this means giving of your excess possessions. I hope you found great joy and satisfaction in donating your unused things to charity, where they can eventually pass into the hands of those who need them most. And I hope you found that generosity brings its own rewards—that you like how it made you feel to give.

Subsequently, you will look for more opportunities to be generous. You will use some of the excess money you have to support causes you believe in. You'll use the availability you've created in your schedule to serve and volunteer.

Become more generous. I've never met a generous person who wasn't enjoying the practice.

5. Look for a Greater Purpose Outside Yourself

Ultimately, if we're attentive, we'll glimpse a greater peak in the distance—one we may not have seen when we began this journey. It's a purpose beyond ourselves. A purpose bigger than ourselves. One that's worthy of the life we've been given to live.

For some, this purpose is centered on their family: their spouse, kids, parents, or other relatives.

For others, this may be a specific cause: the homeless, the environment, animals, children, the disabled, addicts, or something else.

Still others might discover that in their career or work they are able to find greater purpose by serving others and not merely earning a paycheck.

What passion burns within you? What opportunities present themselves? What needs do you have the ability to meet?

Enjoy the personal rewards of minimizing your home, by all means. But go further to look for and attach yourself to purposes outside yourself.

6. Get Moving

Earlier in this book, I described a home as both a safe haven from the storms of life and a port of departure into experiences of greater service and significance. That means *you're* the ship. And a ship is meant to move.

Eventually you've got to cast off the mooring line and set sail. Sign up as the coach on your daughter's softball team. Fill out the volunteer application at the nonprofit downtown. Tell the registrar you're ready to resume your college studies.

We make progress only when we're moving.

True, you may never reach the destination you have in mind. You may change course not once but many times, accomplishing different things from what you originally intended. But only a ship in motion can reorient its navigation. And often the new opportunities we discover as we're heading somewhere else are actually better than we could ever have anticipated.

The How of the What

As I write this, my maternal grandfather, Harold Salem, is ninety-six years old and still working full time with a television ministry that reaches most of the world. My grandmother, Beulah Salem, passed away on Christmas Eve 2007. They lived most of their lives in Aberdeen, South Dakota—the town where I learned there is no place like home.

When I was growing up in Aberdeen, my grandfather was the pastor of the church we attended. Later in life I would come to admire his preaching, but when I was young, I would often get bored during the service. Whenever that happened, I would tell my mom that I needed to go to the bathroom. Actually, I wanted to be with my grandma.

After escaping from the sanctuary, I would find Grandma in the nursery. She would usually be sitting peacefully in a rocking chair, rocking a baby to sleep with a sweet and contented expression on her face. (I've never met another woman so gifted at comforting and quieting a crying child—or relieving the nerves of an anxious mother.) I would ask her if she needed help, and she would say no but would invite me to stay with her and keep her company.

While we lingered in the nursery, a black-and-white television screen on the wall would be showing my grandfather preaching. His sermons were broadcast live around the country, and eventually around the world, from the sanctuary I had just walked out of. Grandma watched the sermons faithfully every week from that church nursery, surrounded by little ones.

I remember so well the contrast:

- my grandfather up on stage, the center of attention, preaching to the masses
- my grandmother in a rocking chair, hidden in a small room down a hallway, caring for one sleeping baby at a time

Which of the pair was serving others?

Both of them!

I believe that a minimalist life should be a mission-forward life. That mission may be "big"—daring, visible, attention grabbing. But it doesn't have to be. Things that seem "small" can be big in impact too if you do them in love and humility.

In fact, just as minimalism makes us contrarian in the way we approach material ownership, so I believe it should make us different in the way we approach our pursuit of goals. Whether we are checking off a bucket-list item (climbing Mount Kilimanjaro), making the transition to a different lifestyle (leaving the office to sell homemade crafts online), or leading a crusade to bring some kind of service to humanity (fighting child abuse), we do it not for applause but because it's a good thing in itself. And I hope we do it while exhibiting such virtues as kindness, compassion, sympathy, wisdom, prudence, modesty, fairness, and humor. These are the kinds of virtues we draw nearer to when we spurn materialism's harsher values of greed, acquisitiveness, and showing off. But we must nurture the loving qualities in our hearts to make them grow and become fruitful.

So the simple correlative to my call for all of us to go after our dreams is this: The *what* (our goals and purposes) is crucial, to be sure. But the *how* matters just as much.

Next Generation, New World

I was sitting in a Colorado radio studio in the middle of recording an interview when the interviewer said he wanted to play an audio clip for me. I was stunned to hear my daughter's voice coming over the speakers. She was responding to a question about how her father's passion for minimalism had influenced her life. "I learned that I don't need as much stuff as I think I do," then-eleven-year-old Alexa said. "Because you think you need all this stuff, but you don't actually end up using most of it."

I hadn't known that the program producers had already spoken with Alexa by phone to get a quote for use in my interview. Her voice in the clip caught me by surprise. And I'll confess, I got a little choked up as I listened to her words, though I had to cover it quickly in order to continue with the conversation.

As I have reflected on my emotional reaction to her words, I think there were two reasons why I was so moved.

First, I felt fatherly pride in having instilled my own priority of minimalism in Alexa. There are many values I hope to pass along to my kids. Among them, the emptiness of accumulating material possessions ranks near the top. At eleven, Alexa already "got it"—she knew that having too many goods isn't good.

Second, and more important, when I realized that Alexa really understood the truths of minimalism, it told me she was poised to accomplish great things in her life. And I know it's the same for her brother, Salem. Because they are not clinging to material things, a whole world is open to them, full of wonderful things they can pursue, experience, and achieve. They might not always take hold of the opportunities they have, but those opportunities are there for them. They only have to reach out and seize them.

I believe minimalism will change everything for my children and for multitudes from their generation in nations all around the world.

May it do the same for you, starting today.

Acknowledgments

From the moment my neighbor first introduced me to the word *minimalism* to the final word written on an airplane somewhere between Reykjavík and New York City, *The Minimalist Home* is a book ten years in the making. Both directly and indirectly, this book is a result of those who have spoken into my life.

First and foremost, I owe the biggest thanks that can ever be communicated on paper to Eric Stanford, my writing partner on this project. Eric was the editor on my first book with WaterBrook, *The More of Less,* and my only requirement for this book was that he be assigned to my project again. Amid missed deadlines, half-finished sentences, and barely rough outlines, Eric showed grace and confidence and even a willingness to accept a far greater role than previously imagined. As before, I'm a better person after working with him. And this book is ten thousand times better.

Thank you also to my publisher, particularly Susan Tjaden and Tina Constable, for pushing my writing in this direction. Thank you also to my agent, Christopher Ferebee, for your support and guidance. This book is helpful and important. Thank you for your boldness in steering my writing toward it.

Thank you also to the tens of thousands of people who have participated in the Uncluttered course. Your stories and questions, comments and emails have brought real-life examples and experiences to my ideas. You have shaped the principles contained inside this book. And your success has inspired me.

Most importantly, thank you to my family to whom this book is dedicated. Thank you to my parents for modeling a healthy, loving family relationship—no doubt you will credit your parents for doing the same for you. And thank you to my wife and kids, Kim, Salem, and Alexa, for supporting me in my work and my endeavors. Wherever my work and passion take me, home will always be my favorite place to be.

Notes

Chapter 1: Minimalism Makeover

1. Frank Trentmann, *Empire of Things: How We Became a World of Consumers, from the Fifteenth Century to the Twenty-First* (New York: HarperCollins, 2016), 683.

2. Mark Whitehouse, "Number of the Week: Americans Buy More Stuff They Don't Need," *Wall Street Journal,* April 23, 2011, https://blogs.wsj.com/economics/2011/04/23/number-of-the-week-americans-buy-more-stuff-they-dont-need/.

3. Marni Jameson, "Do You Really Need to Rent That Self-Storage Space?" *Orlando Sentinel,* February 4, 2016, www.orlandosentinel.com/features/home/os-marni-jameson-self-storage-units-20160204-column.html.

4. Self Storage Association, fact sheet, July 1, 2015, www.selfstorage.org/LinkClick.aspx?fileticket=fJYAow6_AU0%3D&portalid=0.

5. Shane Ferro, "47% of American Households Save Nothing," Business Insider, March 24, 2015, www.businessinsider.com/half-of-america-doesnt-save-any-money-2015-3#ixzz3Zv4X3MUR.

6. Worldwatch Institute, "The State of Consumption Today," www.worldwatch.org/node/810.

7. Research and Markets, "Home Organization in the U.S.: General Purpose, Closets, Garages, and Storage Sheds, 4th edition," March 2017, www.researchandmarkets.com/research/qf6j2p/home_organization.

8. "Lost Something Already Today? Misplaced Items Cost Us Ten Minutes a Day," Daily Mail (UK), March 20, 2012, www.dailymail.co.uk/news/article-2117987/Lost-today-Misplaced-items-cost-minutes-day.html.

9. Steve Howard, "IKEA Executive on Why the West Has Hit 'Peak Stuff,'" interview by Ari Shapiro, National Public Radio, January 22,

2016, www.npr.org/2016/01/22/464013718/ikea-executive-on-why
-the-west-has-hit-peak-stuff.

10. "Most Watched Movies of All Time," IMDb, www.imdb.com/list
/ls053826112/. Like *The Wizard of Oz, E.T.* is also about going home.

11. John A. Shedd, *The Yale Book of Quotations,* ed. Fred R. Shapiro (New
Haven, CT: Yale University Press, 2006), 705.

Chapter 2: The Becker Method

1. Joshua Becker, *Clutterfree with Kids: Change Your Thinking, Discover New
Habits, Free Your Home* (Peoria, AZ: Becoming Minimalist, 2014), 170.

Chapter 3: "Us" Rooms

1. Paul Emrath, "Spaces in New Homes," National Association of Home
Builders, October 1, 2013, www.nahb.org/en/research/housing
-economics/special-studies/spaces-in-new-homes-2013.aspx.

2. Guilia M. Dotti Sani and Judith Treas, "Educational Gradients in
Parents' Child-Care Time Across Countries, 1965–2012," *Journal
of Marriage and Family* 78, no. 4 (August 2016): 1083–96.

Chapter 4: Personal Refuge

1. Lisa Esposito, "To Sleep Better, Stay Cool and Cut Clutter," *U.S. News
and World Report,* December 30, 2015, https://health.usnews.com
/health-news/health-wellness/articles/2015-12-30/to-sleep-better-stay
-cool-and-cut-clutter.

2. Paul Emrath, "Size of New Homes Continues to Edge Up," National
Association of Home Builders, August 14, 2013, http://eyeonhousing
.org/2013/08/size-of-new-homes-continues-to-edge-up/.

3. "Average Number of People Per Family in the United States from 1960
to 2016," Statista, www.statista.com/statistics/183657/average-size-of
-a-family-in-the-us/.

4. Ovid, *Ars Amatoria*, II. 351.

5. Ferris Jabr, "Why Your Brain Needs More Downtime," *Scientific American*, October 15, 2013, www.scientificamerican.com/article /mental-downtime/.

6. John Koblin, "How Much Do We Love TV? Let Us Count the Ways," *New York Times*, June 30, 2016, www.nytimes.com/2016/07/01 /business/media/nielsen-survey-media-viewing.html?mcubz=0.

7. Jessica Schmerler, "Q&A: Why Is Blue Light Before Bedtime Bad for Sleep?" *Scientific American*, September 1, 2015, www.scientificamerican .com/article/q-a-why-is-blue-light-before-bedtime-bad-for-sleep/.

8. Paul C. Rosenblatt, *Two in a Bed: The Social System of Couple Bed Sharing* (Albany: State University of New York Press, 2006), 9–10.

9. "TV's a Bedroom Turn-Off," *Manchester Evening News* (UK), updated January 12, 2013, www.manchestereveningnews.co.uk/news/greater -manchester-news/tvs-a-bedroom-turn-off-1016884.

10. Jessica Kelmon, "Is There a TV in Your Child's Room?" Great Schools, October 28, 2016, www.greatschools.org/gk/articles/effects-of-tv-in -children-bedroom/; and "Study Finds Children with Electronics in Their Bedrooms Get Less Sleep," *Huffington Post*, January 6, 2015, www.huffingtonpost.com/2015/01/06/children-electronics-sleep_n _6422162.html.

11. "How Much Sleep Do We Really Need?" National Sleep Foundation, https://sleepfoundation.org/how-sleep-works/how-much-sleep-do-we -really-need.

12. Jeffrey M. Jones, "In U.S., 40% Get Less Than Recommended Amount of Sleep," Gallup News, December 19, 2013, http://news.gallup.com /poll/166553/less-recommended-amount-sleep.aspx.

13. "Insufficient Sleep Is a Public Health Problem," Centers for Disease Control and Prevention, updated September 3, 2015, www.cdc.gov /features/dssleep/ (site discontinued).

14. Gwen Dewar, "Sleep Requirements in Children," Parenting Science, last modified January 2014, www.parentingscience.com/sleep-requirements .html.

15. "How Long Is the Average Night's Sleep Around the World?" *Huffington Post,* August 24, 2013, www.huffingtonpost.com/2013/08/24/average -daily-nightly-sleep-country-world_n_3805886.html.

Chapter 5: Iconic

1. Alice Gregory, "Alice Gregory on Finding a Uniform," J. Crew, http:// hello.jcrew.com/2014-10-oct/alice-gregory.

2. Henry David Thoreau, *Walden,* vol. 1 (1854; repr., Boston: Houghton Mifflin, 1897), 43.

3. Matilda Kahl, "Why I Wear the Exact Same Thing to Work Every Day," *Harper's Bazaar,* April 3, 2015, www.harpersbazaar.com /culture/features/a10441/why-i-wear-the-same-thing-to-work -everday/.

4. Paul Emrath, "Spaces in New Homes," National Association of Home Builders, October 1, 2013, www.nahb.org/en/research/housing -economics/special-studies/spaces-in-new-homes-2013.aspx.

5. Samuel Weigley, "11 Home Features Buyers Will Pay Extra For," *USA Today,* April 28, 2013, www.usatoday.com/story/money/personal finance/2013/04/28/24-7-home-features/2106203/.

6. "Pantone Fashion Color Report for Fall 2008," Fashion Trendsetter, www.fashiontrendsetter.com/content/color_trends/2008/Pantone -Fashion-Color-Report-Fall-2008.html#ixzz4YOwFPkko.

7. Emma Johnson, "The Real Cost of Your Shopping Habits," *Forbes,* January 15, 2015, www.forbes.com/sites/emmajohnson/2015/01/15 /the-real-cost-of-your-shopping-habits/#186188151452.

8. Gretchen Frazee, "How to Stop 13 Million Tons of Clothing from Getting Trashed Every Year," *PBS News Hour,* June 7, 2016, www.pbs

.org/newshour/updates/how-to-stop-13-million-tons-of-clothing-from
-getting-trashed-every-year/.

9. Johnson, "The Real Cost of Your Shopping Habits."

10. Frank Trentmann, *Empire of Things: How We Became a World of Consumers, from the Fifteenth Century to the Twenty-First* (New York: HarperCollins, 2016), 674.

11. Sean Poulter, "In Every Woman's Closet, 22 Items She Never Wears—and the Guilt Complex That Stops Them Clearing Wardrobes Out," *Daily Mail* (UK), January 26, 2011, www.dailymail.co.uk/femail/article-1350447/Women-waste-1-6bn-clothes-Guilt-prevents-wardrobe-clear-out.html.

12. Leah Melby Clinton, "This Is What the Average American Woman's Closet Is Worth," *Glamour,* June 25, 2015, www.glamour.com/story/average-worth-of-clothing-owned.

13. Rebecca Adams, "Men Think About Sex Less Than Women Think About Fashion, Survey Says," *Huffington Post,* June 8, 2012, www.huffingtonpost.com/2012/06/08/fashion-study-online-2012_n_1580663.html.

14. Barry Schwartz, *The Paradox of Choice: Why More Is Less,* rev. ed. (New York: Ecco Press, 2016), 103.

15. "Surprising Stats," Simply Orderly, http://simplyorderly.com/surprising-statistics/.

16. Courtney Carver, "Capsule Wardrobe Hacks: 10 Tiny Temporary Tips," Be More with Less, https://bemorewithless.com/capsule-wardrobe-tips/.

17. Quoted in Jon Pierce, *Social Studies: Collected Essays, 1974–2013* (Victoria, BC: Friesen Press, 2014), 205.

Chapter 6: Clean Sweep

1. Ritchie King, "Meet the Prototypical American Home: Three Bedrooms, Two Bathrooms, and Central Air," Quartz, January 4, 2013, https://qz

.com/40707/meet-the-prototypical-american-home-three-bedrooms-two
-bathrooms-and-central-air/; and Paul Emrath, "Size of New Homes
Continues to Edge Up," Eye On Housing, August 14, 2013, http://
eyeonhousing.org/2013/08/size-of-new-homes-continues-to-edge-up/.

2. Myra Butterworth, "An Englishman's Ideal Home Isn't a Castle!" *Daily
Mail* (UK), March 18, 2016, www.dailymail.co.uk/property/article
-3498631/Britons-look-three-bedroom-homes-sale-two-bathrooms
-garden.html; and Danielle Cahill, "What Does Australia's Ideal House
Look Like?" April 16, 2016, www.realestate.com.au/news/what-does
-australias-ideal-house-look-like/.

3. Edward Lewis, "Why Is the Bathroom the Most Important Room in
the House?" LinkedIn, February 23, 2016, www.linkedin.com/pulse
/why-bathroom-most-important-room-house-edward-lewis/.

4. Katie Wells, "Natural Homemade All-Purpose Cleaner (That Works!),"
Wellness Mama, updated February 27, 2018, https://wellnessmama.com
/756/homemade-all-purpose-cleaner/.

5. Katie Wells, "How to Make Laundry Soap (Liquid or Powder Recipe),"
updated March 29, 2018, Wellness Mama, https://wellnessmama.com
/462/homemade-laundry-detergent/.

6. Ann C. Foster, "Household Healthcare Spending in 2014," *Beyond the
Numbers* 5, no. 13 (August 2016), www.bls.gov/opub/btn/volume-5
/household-healthcare-spending-in-2014.htm; and "Statistics on OTC
Use," Consumer Healthcare Productions Association, www.chpa.org
/marketstats.aspx.

7. "Where and How to Dispose of Unused Medicines," US Food and
Drug Administration, October 25, 2017, www.fda.gov/ForConsumers
/ConsumerUpdates/ucm101653.htm.

8. Sam Escobar, "The Number of Makeup Products the Average Woman
Owns Is Just Plain Shocking," *Good Housekeeping,* October 14, 2015,
www.goodhousekeeping.com/beauty/makeup/a34976/average-makeup
-products-owned/.

9. Alexander Fury, "Men's Grooming Is Now a Multi-Billion Pound Worldwide Industry," *Independent* (UK), January 14, 2016, www .independent.co.uk/life-style/fashion/features/mens-grooming-is-now -a-multi-billion-pound-worldwide-industry-a6813196.html.

10. Katherine Ashenburg, "Why Do Americans Cherish Cleanliness? Look to War and Advertising," *New York Times,* May 28, 2013, www.ny times.com/roomfordebate/2013/05/27/are-americans-too-obsessed-with -cleanliness/why-do-americans-cherish-cleanliess-look-to-war-and -advertising.

11. "Toiletry Industry Statistics," Statistic Brain, www.statisticbrain.com /toiletry-soap-industry-statistics/. The statistics are based on research conducted in 2016.

12. Christina Stiehl, "America's Hygiene Obsession Is Expensive and Unhealthy," January 26, 2017, Thrillist, www.thrillist.com/health/nation /expensive-american-hygiene-obsession.

Chapter 7: The Heart of the Home

1. Ayelet Fishbach, quoted in Shankar Vedantam, "Why Eating the Same Food Increases People's Trust and Cooperation," interview by David Greene, NPR, February 2, 2017, www.npr.org/2017/02/02/512998465 /why-eating-the-same-food-increases-peoples-trust-and-cooperation.

2. Frank Trentmann, *Empire of Things: How We Became a World of Consumers, from the Fifteenth Century to the Twenty-First* (New York: HarperCollins, 2016), 674.

3. "Major Domestic Appliances Unit Sales Worldwide from 2006 to 2016 (in Millions)," Statista, www.statista.com/statistics/539974/major -domestic-appliances-unit-sales-worldwide/.

4. Heather Long, "23% of American Homes Have Two (Or More) Fridges," CNN Money, May 27, 2016, http://money.cnn.com/2016/05 /27/news/economy/23-percent-of-american-homes-have-2-fridges/index .html.

5. Larisa Brown, "Revealed, Kitchen Gadgets That We Never End Up Using: Every Toastie and Coffee We Make Costs Us £10.68," *Daily Mail* (UK), February 6, 2013, www.dailymail.co.uk/news/article -2274770/Revealed-kitchen-gadgets-end-using-Every-toastie-coffee -make-costs-10-68.html.

6. Mark Bittman, "A No-Frills Kitchen Still Cooks," *New York Times,* May 9, 2007, www.nytimes.com/2007/05/09/dining/09 mini.html.

7. Bittman, "A No-Frills Kitchen Still Cooks."

8. United States Census Bureau, "2013 Housing Profile: United States," May 2015, www2.census.gov/programs-surveys/ahs/2013/factsheets /ahs13-1_UnitedStates.pdf.

9. Tim Chester, *A Meal with Jesus: Discovering Grace, Community, and Mission Around the Table* (Wheaton, IL: Crossway, 2011), 94.

Chapter 8: Freeing the Mind

1. Richard Eisenberg, "Secrets of Claiming a Home Office Deduction," *Forbes,* February 8, 2013, www.forbes.com/sites/nextavenue/2013/02 /08/secrets-of-claiming-a-home-office-deduction/#6e70e45c37a4.

2. Niraj Chokshi, "Out of the Office: More People Are Working Remotely, Survey Finds," *New York Times,* February 15, 2017, www.nytimes.com /2017/02/15/us/remote-workers-work-from-home.html.

3. Craig Link, "About," Digital Minimalism, https://digitalminimalism .org/about/.

4. "Why Can't We Put Down Our Smartphones?" *60 Minutes,* April 7, 2017, www.cbsnews.com/news/why-cant-we-put-down-our-smartphones -60-minutes/.

5. Julia Naftulin, "Here's How Many Times We Touch Our Phones Every Day," July 13, 2016, Business Insider, www.businessinsider .com/dscout-research-people-touch-cell-phones-2617-times-a-day -2016-7.

Chapter 9: Unburdening Yourself of the Past

1. Mary MacVean, "For Many People, Gathering Possessions Is Just the Stuff of Life," *Los Angeles Times,* March 21, 2014, http://articles.latimes.com/2014/mar/21/health/la-he-keeping-stuff-20140322.
2. "Pet Ownership," Global GfK Survey, May 2016, www.gfk.com/fileadmin/user_upload/website_content/Global_Study/Documents/Global-GfK-survey_Pet-Ownership_2016.pdf.
3. Amelia Josephson, "America's Pets by the Numbers: How Much We Spend on Our Animal Friends," LearnVest, February 15, 2016, www.learnvest.com/2016/02/americas-pets-by-the-numbers-how-much-we-spend-on-our-animal-friends.
4. Francine Jay, "Declutter Your Fantasy Self," *Huffington Post,* April 28, 2016, www.huffingtonpost.co.uk/francine-jay/declutter-your-fantasy-self_b_9785190.html.
5. Carly Dauch, Michelle Imwalle, Brooke Ocasio, and Alexia E. Metz, "The Influence of the Number of Toys in the Environment on Toddlers' Play," *Infant Behavior and Development* 50, no. 2 (February 2018): 78–87.

Chapter 10: Your Second Chance to Make a First Impression

1. William Ashdown, "Confessions of an Automobilist," *Atlantic Monthly,* June 1925, 788–92.
2. "A Brief History of American Garages," Blue Sky Builders, www.blueskybuilders.com/blog/history-american-garages/.
3. "A Brief History of American Garages."
4. Robert Dietz, "Two-Car Garage Most Common in New Homes," Eye On Housing, September 15, 2015, http://eyeonhousing.org/2015/09/two-car-garage-most-common-in-new-homes/.
5. From 2004 to 2014, the number of US garages large enough to hold three or more cars increased from about 19 percent to about 23.5 percent. Dietz, "Two-Car Garage Most Common in New Homes." Meanwhile, the average number of cars per household in the United States peaked at

2.07 in 2007. Angie Schmitt, "The American Cities with the Most Growth in Car-Free Households," Greater Greater Washington, January 21, 2014, https://ggwash.org/view/33531/the-american-cities-with-the -most-growth-in-car-free-households. Today there are 1.9 cars per household in the United States. "Household, Individual, and Vehicle Characteristics," Bureau of Transportation Statistics, www.rita.dot.gov/bts /sites/rita.dot.gov.bts/files/publications/highlights_of_the_2001_national _household_travel_survey/html/section_01.html (site discontinued).

6. Gladiator GarageWorks, "Almost 1 in 4 Americans Say Their Garage Is Too Cluttered to Fit Their Car," Cision, June 9, 2015, www.prnewswire .com/news-releases/almost-1-in-4-americans-say-their-garage-is-too -cluttered-to-fit-their-car-300096246.html.

7. Mike Allen, "How to Dispose of Hazardous Waste," *Popular Mechanics,* March 28, 2006, www.popularmechanics.com/cars/how-to/a329 /2063646/.

8. Rachel Botsman and Roo Rogers, *What's Mine Is Yours: The Rise of Collaborative Consumption* (New York: HarperCollins, 2010), 83.

9. Ashley Whillans, quoted in Niraj Chokshi, "Want to Be Happy? Buy More Takeout and Hire a Maid, Study Suggests," *New York Times,* July 27, 2017, www.nytimes.com/2017/07/27/science/study-happy-save -money-time.html.

10. United States Census Bureau, "Historical Census of Housing Tables," www.census.gov/hhes/www/housing/census/historic/units.html.

11. Andrew McGill, "The Shrinking of the American Lawn," *Atlantic Monthly,* July 6, 2016, www.theatlantic.com/business/archive/2016/07 /lawns-census-bigger-homes-smaller-lots/489590/.

12. Frank Chung, "Lot Sizes Getting Smaller: The Great Australian Land Grab," September 11, 2014, www.news.com.au/finance/real-estate/ buying/lot-sizes-getting-smaller-the-great-australian-land-grab/news- story/c14408ae4995b9b62a8d37313933f881.

Special Section: Minimalism Maintenance Guide

1. "Holiday 2017," National Retail Federation, https://nrf.com /resources/consumer-research-and-data/holiday-spending/holiday -headquarters.

Chapter 11: A Small Suggestion

1. Christina Hernandez Sherwood, "Becoming Minimalist: When Having Fewer Possessions Means Living a Better Life," August 12, 2010, ZDNet, www.zdnet.com/article/becoming-minimalist-when-having-fewer -possessions-means-living-a-better-life/.

2. Mona Chalabi, "How Many Times Does the Average Person Move?" FiveThirtyEight, January 29, 2015, https://fivethirtyeight.com/features /how-many-times-the-average-person-moves/.

3. United States Census Bureau, "Americans Moving at Historically Low Rates," press release, November 16, 2016, https://census.gov/newsroom /press-releases/2016/cb16-189.html.

4. United States Census Bureau, "Median and Average Square Feet of Floor Area in New Single- Family Houses Completed by Location," www.census.gov/const/C25Ann/sftotalmedavgsqft.pdf.

5. Mark J. Perry, "New U.S. Homes Today Are 1,000 Square Feet Larger Than in 1973 and Living Space Per Person Has Nearly Doubled," AEI, June 5, 2016, www.aei.org/publication/new-us-homes-today-are-1000 -square-feet-larger-than-in-1973-and-living-space-per-person-has-nearly -doubled/.

6. "Average Number of People Per Household in the United States from 1960 to 2016," Statista, www.statista.com/statistics/183648/average -size-of-households-in-the-us/.

7. Ralph McLaughlin, "Americans (Can't Get No) Home Size Satisfac- tion," Trulia, March 1, 2017, www.trulia.com/blog/trends/home-size -survey-march-16/.

8. Lindsay Wilson, "How Big Is a House? Average House Size by Country," Shrink That Footprint, http://shrinkthatfootprint.com/how-big-is-a -house.

9. Drew Desilver, "As American Homes Get Bigger, Energy Efficiency Gains Are Wiped Out," Pew Research Center, November 9, 2015, www.pewresearch.org/fact-tank/2015/11/09/as-american-homes-get -bigger-energy-efficiency-gains-are-wiped-out/.

10. Bureau of Labor Statistics, US Department of Labor, "Consumer Expenditures—2016," press release, August 29, 2017, www.bls.gov /news.release/pdf/cesan.pdf.

11. Alan Pyke, "Americans Already Spent a Shocking Amount on Rent, But It Just Got Worse," Think Progress, August 13, 2015, https:// thinkprogress.org/americans-already-spent-a-shocking-amount-on-rent -but-it-just-got-worse-df2ba23a0a6d/.

12. "U.S. Existing Home Median Sales Price," Y Charts, https://ycharts.com /indicators/sales_price_of_existing_homes.

13. "Average Monthly Mortgage Payments," Value Penguin, www.value penguin.com/mortgages/average-monthly-mortgage-payment.

14. Clare Trapasso, "Homeowners Spent a Record Amount on Remodeling—but on What, Exactly?" Realtor.com, February 28, 2017, www.realtor.com/news/trends/home owners-spend-record-amount-on -remodeling/; and "List of Countries by Projected GDP," Statistics Times, April 23, 2017, http://statisticstimes.com/economy/countries -by-projected-gdp.php.

15. For the purposes of this chart, I am making the following assumptions: median cost to buy a home of $123 per square foot; mortgage payment at rate of 4.25 percent for thirty-year fixed loan; mortgage insurance of 1 percent annual on mortgage value; monthly property tax of 1.15 percent; monthly utility expense of $1.68 per square foot; monthly maintenance cost roughly based on 1 percent of home value.

16. Charlotte Local, quoted in Valencia Higuera, "15 Reasons You Need to Downsize Your Home," Go Banking Rates, October 15, 2017, www.gobankingrates.com/investing/reasons-need-downsize-home/.

17. Trulia, "8 Reasons to Buy a 1000-Square-Foot House," *Forbes,* June 15, 2016.

18. Originally published as "Why We Rent," *What If We Fly,* April 14, 2016, www.whatifweflyblog.com/?p=219&. Adapted and used by permission.

19. Ama Otet, "As US Apartments Get Smaller, Atlanta, Charlotte, Boston Rank Among Top Cities with Largest Rental Units," Rent Café Blog, June 23, 2016, www.rentcafe.com/blog/rental-market/us-average-apartment-size-trends-downward/.

20. Tom de Castella, "A Life Lived in Tiny Flats," *BBC News Magazine,* April 19, 2013, www.bbc.com/news/magazine-22152622.

Chapter 12: This Changes Everything

1. Scott Barry Kaufman, "The Differences Between Happiness and Meaning in Life," *Scientific American,* January 30, 2016, https://blogs.scientificamerican.com/beautiful-minds/the-differences-between-happiness-and-meaning-in-life/.

2. Patrick L. Hill and Nicholas A. Turiano, "Purpose in Life as a Predictor of Mortality Across Adulthood," *Psychological Science* 25, no. 7 (May 8, 2014): 1482–6.

The ultimate guide on
what to keep, what to get rid of,
and how to make room
for your dreams.

An empowering plan for living more by owning less. With practical suggestions and encouragement to personalize your own minimalist style, Joshua Becker shows you why *minimizing* possessions is the best way to *maximize* life.